SUPERMAN IS AN IDIOT

SUPERMAN IS AN IDIOT

By
The Very Reverend Angus J. MacQueen,
B.A., B.D., D.D., LL.D.

SERMONS AND ADDRESSES

LANCELOT PRESS
Windsor, Nova Scotia

DEDICATION

This Book is for Netta

ISBN   0-88999-063-8

Published 1976

LANCELOT PRESS LIMITED, Windsor, N. S.

CONTENTS

FOREWORD

A sermon is not a creation of literary art but "an intimate conversational message from soul to soul", and is therefore designed to be heard rather than to be read. These sermons and addresses have, for the most part, been taken from tapes, and still retain much of the style of the spoken word. Since they are productions of a busy parish minister and not of a homiletical specialist, they are published with some misgiving. They appear in this more permanent form at the request of appreciative listeners. Over the years I have been fortunate to have congregations which respected the role of the preacher and his study hours.

In the Acts of the Apostles (5:20) we are told that an angel of God bade Peter and John and the other Apostles to "Go and stand and speak in the temple, and tell the people all about this new life", in Jesus Christ. What an awesome responsibility, and privilege, for frail human beings! Not just to pass along the wisdom of the village philosopher, the panaceas of the amateur psychologist, the pep-talks of the religious booster, the erudition of the theologian, or the diagnosis and call-to-arms of the social reformer, but to communicate the "Word of Life" — in all its fullness and freedom, challenge and promise. Despite the enormity of the task and my own inadequacy to perform it, I feel sorry for my friends who are not preachers!

My warm appreciation is expressed to Mrs. Joan Eichner, our church librarian, and Mrs. Vi Davis, my secretary, for their careful typing of the manuscript. Mrs. Eichner has also made helpful suggestions on the choice of material and in many instances spared me from letting loose on my readers awkward and ill-chosen construction. My major indebtedness, however, is to my wife, Netta, who has always been my most truthful and trustworthy critic.

I

SUPERMAN IS AN IDIOT

(Tower of Babel)

Then they said: "Come let us build ourselves a city, and a tower with its top in the heavens, and let us make a name for ourselves."

Genesis 11:4

Twenty years ago, in 1953, an American scientist, Dr. C. L. Farar, Head of the Department of Agriculture's bee laboratory in Madison, Wisconsin, succeeded in breeding what he called "Superbees", the largest bees known. He tells us that they are fantastic honey producers, and are very resistant to disease. There is only one catch, namely, that the Superbees have a supersting, and Dr. Farar and his assistants get on an average 2000 stings a day.

Dr. Farar with his Superbees is not an oddball but is typical of our age. Everything in our world has to be super. It's super-this or super-that — a craze for the biggest. Everything must be bigger than its predecessors and its competitors. Samuel Goldwin, the famous film-maker, said that one night he had a dream of the perfect film, which opened with an earthquake and worked up to a climax. A C.B.S. newsman tells about going into a store in Hollywood to buy a tube of toothpaste. He went up to the clerk at the counter and asked for a small tube; she handed him a tube with the word "large" written on it. He objected and said he had asked for a small tube, not a large one. She replied: "Sir, we only have the three sizes: large, giant, and super. So if you want a small size, you've got to ask for a large." That's typical of the age and culture in which we live!

Some years ago P. T. Barnum had the largest elephant in captivity, and they called him "Jumbo". He may have had other fine qualities, but this was the only one that really mattered, namely, that he was the biggest elephant in captivity.

And so "jumboism" has come to mean, "the craze or mania for the biggest", for the super — for the biggest car, the biggest salary, the biggest city, the biggest Church, etc. And our age has produced such super things as the military-industrial complex that we see in the United States; the super-giant corporations which cross international boundary lines and carry more weight and punch than most of the nations of the world (General Motors, U.S. Steel, Alcan, etc.); super-political units, seen in the great power blocs, in N.A.T.O., and in totalitarian states — omni-competent, omni-present, and omnipotent; super-trade-unions which also cross international borders with ease, and which can not only paralyse a giant corporation but also a whole nation; super-spy-systems, as seen in the C.I.A. in the United States and in its Russian counterpart, and on a smaller scale in Watergate, with the Haldemans and Erlichmans and Deans; and the most terrifying of all these colossi of power — the super-bomb. We are living in an age which has a mania for the biggest, and our bombs must be bigger than all their predecessors and competitors.

This craze is as old as the human race, going back to the first man Adam. Adam "fell" or sinned because he wanted to be a superman. We read in *Genesis* that Adam and Eve wanted to be like God. We find the same desire in the story of the Tower of Babel. "Babel" stands for Babylon: it is the Hebrew form. The earliest civilization on earth was in Lower Mesopotamia and the area of Babylon, and was already a developed civilization by 3500 B.C., whereas the civilization in Egypt dates to about 3000 B.C., in India about 2500 B.C., in China about 1500 B.C.; the Incas and other civilizations of South America being even later. But according to great archeologists such as Albright and Finegan, and great historians such as Breasted, this was the first civilization on earth: the one in the Lower Mesopotamia, in the Fertile Crescent area. Babel is the name of that Babylonian or Sumerian civilization.

The mark of that civilization was like that of ours and all other urban civilizations, an impressive city with a high tower. The Bible reports that the inhabitants said: "Let us build us a city and a tower which will reach as high as heaven, and let us make us a name." That sounds pretty modern. The ruins of ancient towers can still be found in that area of the world. They were quite huge — some of them as much as 300 feet square at the base, going high up in seven different terraced storeys, with a shrine at the top, rising three hundred or more feet in the air. That was quite a height for the year 3500 B.C. The George Washington Tower in Washington is only 555 feet high. Toronto, with its new CN Tower of 1815 feet, makes all of these look pretty insignificant.

At any rate the people came together and built a city, and a Ziggurat with a high tower and shrine and temple, and they made themselves a name. But when they had done all this, as the story goes, God came thundering down and confused all the inhabitants so that they spoke different languages and could not understand one another. The result was chaos and confusion and disaster.

This is one of the great stories in human literature. Let us not be put off by some of the details, and some of the historical and scientific and theological difficulties. Of course God is not a big man sitting on a throne up in the sky, who, at times when he gets annoyed or jealous, comes thundering from His throne down to earth and despoils things. And heaven isn't "up"; there is no such place in the universe as "up" or "down", because the globe on which we live goes round and round, and what is up now is down in a few hours' time. And of course there never was a day in the history of mankind when all human beings spoke one language, and that language brought harmony and peace, so that it was necessary for God to create a confusion of tongues to prevent men from becoming a threat to Him. No, let's not be put off by these difficulties in science and theology, but let us notice the tremendous truths in the story of the Tower of Babel.

1) It was a primitive attempt to explain the diversity of languages and tongues throughout the whole world, and to point out that this diversity created all kinds of misunderstandings and suspicions, and, indeed, human conflict. We know that this sort of thing is true in our own country: division and misunderstanding are caused by language barriers. Anyone who has ever visited the new countries of Africa, with all their tribal languages, and deep misunderstandings, also sees the difficulties. When you go to the United Nations General Assembly, you notice that if there is to be any understanding and harmony at all, there has to be some means of overcoming the linguistic problem, and so there is made available simultaneous translation in at least six or seven languages.

2) Man is always trying to act bigger than he is. He wants to be autonomous. He resents God, and God's authority over him, and God's claim upon him. He is always ready to rebel against God and to clench his fist in God's face. He wants to run his own show. This is true of each one of us — men and women, boys and girls — we each want to be autonomous.

The ancient Hebrews understood this well, in their stories of Adam and Eve, and of the Tower of Babel. The ancient Greeks understood it too, in their story of Prometheus, who battered heaven and stole fire, bringing it down to earth.

And in the story of Icarus, whose father, the skilful artificer, made wings for himself and his son, and fastened them on with wax, and told the boy not to fly too high, or close to the sun, for the heat of the sun would melt the wax on the wings and he would come to disaster. But the boy, being human, could not resist the temptation, and as he flew with more and more skill, like Jonathan Livingston Seagull, higher and higher, he came too near the sun, and the wax melted and he came plummeting down into the sea. All you could hear was the cry and then the lament of his father, as he saw the feathers floating on the surface of the ocean. The Greeks, like the Hebrews, understood that man's primeval and perennial sin is his *hubris*, his pride — his desire to take over and run his own life and the lives of other people. This pride, or self-centredness, is what sets him against God and against his fellowman: creating isolation, rebellion, alienation, jealousy, mistrust, and conflict.

The writer of *Proverbs* agreed, and said a man's pride will bring him low: "Pride goeth before destruction and a haughty spirit before a fall." John Milton understood it. In *Paradise Lost* he pictures Lucifer, the great devil, being cast out of heaven because of his pride and rebellion against God. The philosopher Nietzche stated the problem this way: "If there were a God, I could not endure not being He." Even Jean-Paul Sartre, the modern French existentialist, who does not believe in God, has said: "Every man aspires to be like a God." This is what the story of the Tower of Babel is telling us — that every man tries to act bigger than he is, every man tries to impress the world with his name and works, every man wants to play Superman; and that it is man's pride that destroys his greatest achievements, and turns his noblest victories into his worst vices.

In other words, man's greatest evil is the corruption of the good. This is true with individuals: man's worst sin, self-righteousness, comes because of his moral victories and virtues. Man somehow or other cannot stand success. He

11

becomes puffed up, and feels righteous within himself, as some of the Pharisees did in Jesus' day.

It is the same story with corporate man, and caused the tragedy of the Babylonian Empire, Egyptian civilization, ancient Greece with all its wealth and power and culture and philosophy, and the mightiest of them all, Imperial Rome. We now refer to the glory that *was* Greece and the grandeur that *was* Rome, and men cast their fishing nets over ancient Tyre and Sidon, and dig for artifacts among the ruins of Persia and Babylon. Pride brought all these nations low. They fell from a great height because of their presumption, self-worship, and self-satisfaction.

3) Surely this means that when man plays Superman, he is an idiot. "Idiot" means "fool" — one who doesn't understand, doesn't see clearly, doesn't discern, doesn't comprehend. His own self-importance blinds him to certain elementary truths, and perils.

a) Superman mistakes "super" for "superior". Therefore he thinks that the bigger a thing is the better it is. H. G. Wells felt this way. Once commenting on the Bible and the ancient stories, he dismissed Solomon's Temple with the remark "Many a modern barn is bigger than Solomon's Temple." Bigger — therefore better. By this way of thinking, a full-grown elephant is better than a baby; a majority vote counts for more than excellence, truth, and spiritua' awareness; and the big things of our materialistic culture are more important than the small and unobtrusive values of the conscience and soul of man.

b) Superman fails to see the super-possibilities of evil in his super-creations. To go back to the story with which we began, the story of Dr. C. L. Farar and the Superbee — the trouble with the Superbee is that it has super-possibilities of evil. It has a super-sting. Isn't this the trouble with super political units, and super-corporations, super-unions, super-spy organizations, super-bombs? During the last part of the 19th century and the early part of the 20th, Western man was pretty naive. He believed that all his great inventions and technological progress and fine achievements would one day bring him to Utopia, that he could construct a perfect society here on earth because he had the intelligence, the inventive genius, and all the good will in the world; that he was a reasonable, decent and beneficent creature.

That naive presumption gets no support from the Bible. The Bible does not say that man is either reasonable or beneficent. Neither does human history say so. And since 1914 the liberal delusion has been knocked into a cocked hat — by the First World War, the global economic depression of the 30's, the rise of Fascist, Nazi, and Communist organizations across the face of the earth, with their blood purges, gas ovens and all kinds of bestiality, and then by the Second World War with all its fury, ending with the super-bombs of Hiroshima and Nagasaki. When men begin to play Superman they fail to see the super-possibilities of evil, in all their inventions, great creations, and fine achievements which are morally and socially ambivalent or ambiguous.

c) Superman is an idiot because he doesn't understand the nature of power. Lord Acton made it very clear in his statement which has become a proverb, that "power tends to corrupt, and absolute power corrupts absolutely." History teaches us that this is true. We have seen it in the Bible's stories. Saul was a graceful, brilliant, generous young man until he became King and had sovereign power in Israel. Then power corrupted him and his life-story ended as a dismal tragedy. Power corrupted Samson and brought ruin on himself and all around him. And power made a fool of the wise man, Solomon. Outside the Bible, history is a record of the corruption of power in the Babylonians and Egyptians and Romans, and in the mediaeval kings and dynasties; and in such notable figures as Charlemagne, Henry VIII, Napoleon, Hitler and Joseph Stalin. It is the same story in the Church, and religious organizations. Why is it that Pope John XXIII stands out as a great hero of the 20th century? Because he was an exception in the Papal hierarchy — a man of humility. And why is it that so many decent clergymen become insufferable when they are elevated to the rank of Bishop? Power tends to corrupt and absolute power corrupts absolutely. Whether he is in a political, scientific, business, or religious organization, Superman always forgets the dangers of excessive power.

d) Superman takes for granted that the future belongs to him. Nature does not agree. Many aeons ago in the physical world in a time of volcanoes, eruptions, terrible powers, glaciers, etc., there could be found along the water's edge protoplasm, microscopic, tiny, invisible. If you and I had been there and were asked to bet whether the future belonged to the great forces or to the invisible protoplasm, we would have laid our money on the super-powers. But history tells us that we would have been mistaken. The great super-powers disappeared while the protoplasm produced life, from which eventually came human life. From that invisible, microscopic little thing along the water's edge in prehistoric times, came spirit and mind, art and music, science and philosophy and religion.

Christianity also says that God makes the weak things of the world to "confound the mighty." In the early Christian community there were not many noble, not many mighty, not many wise, not many great — just humble, ordinary, commonplace individuals, artisans and tax collectors and fishermen. But somehow or other the future belonged to them and not to Caesar Augustus, or to the mighty Roman Empire, or to the superpowers throughout the world which challenged it. Superman in his idiocy forgets all this, and needs the story of the Tower of Babel to remind him that he is putting his faith in vain things such as "reeking tube and iron shard", and not in the durable forces in God's universe.

14

e) Finally, one of the marks of Superman is that he thinks he no longer needs God. This is the essence of idiocy, because it is the denial of his creatureliness and fallibility, his finiteness and sin, and a declaration of his omniscience, omnicompetence, moral trustworthiness, if not innocence. It flies in the face of both anthropology and history, as well as of theology. And it also denies man's spiritual nature, which links him with his Creator, and will not permit him to find deep satisfaction in "the things of this world." In the words of St. Augustine: "O God, our hearts are restless until they find their rest in Thee."

When Lord Thomson of Fleet, in 1962, had a visit with Nikita Krushchev, then Premier of the U.S.S.R., Mr. Krushchev in good humour teased him about all his money, and said to him amiably, "You can't take it with you." Lord Thomson retorted, to Mr. Krushchev's vast amazement, "Then I'm not going!"

But Lord Thomson is going. And Mr. Krushchev has already gone. The Superman who thinks he is self-sufficient is a pitiable idiot.

Let us underline the difference between Babel and Bethlehem. The first was man's attempt to assume God's throne; the second was God's condescension to man in identification and service. The first was man's denial of his need of God; the second was God's bequest upon man of sonship and grace. The first was man's tedious construction and futile hope; the second was God bestowing upon man an immortal hope. The first was the bad news of frustration, confusion and defeat; the second was the good news of fulfillment, joy and victory.

Our choice is Babel or Bethlehem, chaos or Christ, death or life.

II

WHAT THE GOSPEL IS — AND IS NOT

I noticed in yesterday's paper that one of the other ministers in the city is also preaching today on "What the Gospel is". Think how lucky you are, that I'm also telling you what it is not!

There are many appropriate texts, but the one I have selected is from St. Paul's first letter to Timothy, the first chapter and the eleventh verse:

Sound doctrine, according to the glorious gospel of the blessed God, which gospel was committed to my trust.

Now the word "gospel" is a very common word with several meanings. The Oxford dictionary tells us that it means, in the first place, "a principle, on which one is prepared to act". For example, we talk about the gospel of efficiency, or the gospel of "laissez-faire", or the gospel of socialism. A second meaning is "something that may be safely believed, something credible", for example: "It is the gospel truth". The third meaning for the term "gospel" refers to one of the four books by the four evangelists, Matthew, Mark, Luke and John, which we find in the New Testament. These are four pen-portraits of our Lord and Master, Jesus Christ.

The fourth meaning, which is the important and the original meaning for the word "gospel" comes from two Old English words — "God-spel": the God-story, or the good story.

In Greek it was the word for "evangel" which originally meant "the bearer of good tidings", but later came to refer to the good tidings themselves, the message that the bearer of good tidings brought. In the New Testament, the word "gospel" occurs 72 times and in various forms: the "good news of God", the "good news of Jesus Christ", the "good news of truth", the "good news of grace", the "good news of salvation", the "good news of the cross", the "good news of life". In every occurrence it has the same reference and the same meaning — namely, the message that came to the world from God in Jesus Christ our Lord.

And so, to the early Christians, the gospel was their *raison d'etre*, and their real busines. The Church, the evangelists, the apostles and preachers were all in the business of proclaiming and witnessing to and promoting the gospel. It was a gospel for the whole world, and every man who believed it was to proclaim it. The urgency of this comes through when we read *The Acts of the Apostles* and the *Epistles* of St. Paul and others. The only justification for a preacher standing in a Christian pulpit during the hour of Divine worship was that he should proclaim this gospel. He was not there as a commentator on international affairs, a lecturer on ethics or philosophy, a dabbler in pseudo-psychology or an expert in the art of successful living. These things were not his business. His business was the proclamation of the gospel. The services of Christian worship, and the celebration of the Christian sacraments, were also committed to proclaiming the gospel — to enact it, and show it forth in a powerful and dramatic fashion. This was their business too.

And this is our business as a Church, when we come to worship. It isn't just celebration. We've heard so much talk about "celebration", but we don't come here to celebrate celebration. And we don't come to celebrate religion-in-general, a vague religiosity, spirituality, truth-in-general, idealism, or mysticism. Neither do we come to celebrate life, or

17

nature, or humanity, or social togetherness. We come to celebrate the good news from God in Jesus Christ our Lord. And therefore as a worshipping congregation, and as ministers, we are in business for one reason: the gospel of our Lord Jesus Christ.

A

Well, if that is so, then we should know what the gospel is. Dr. Paul Scherer, a preacher *par excellence* in North America for many years, shortly before his death in 1969, wrote that most people in our generation have never really heard the gospel. He was not referring to the so-called "heathen", but to the so-called "Christians" who go to church. It is they who have not really heard the gospel. They have only heard a *Reader's Digest* version of it, with a little bit of psychology, moralism, and admonitions on Mother's Day, the United Nations, and conciliation — but they have not really heard the gospel.

What is the gospel, then? Before we can say what it is, we must first of all see what it is not.

1) The gospel is not a code of high and heroic morals. Some years ago I got a book called *The Gospel in the Ten Commandments* from a retired minister's library. But there is no gospel in the Ten Commandments! They are good advice, not good news. You don't leap with joy and a sense of gratitude when you read the Ten Commandments! There is no gospel in the Golden Rule, or in the Sermon on the Mount! Nor is there gospel in the Great Commandment: "Thou shalt love the Lord thy God with all thy heart... and thy neighbour as thyself". That is not the gospel! Jesus made that plain when he said that it was the sum of "the Law and the prophets". It is an imperative: but, as Paul Scherer says, the imperative without the indicative that "God so loved the world..." is hopeless, and without any visible means of support.

Charles Haddon Spurgeon, one of the greatest

18

preachers of the nineteenth century, told a story about a friend, a brother minister, who lived in England in a rather poor area. There was a woman in his parish who was always on the edge of poverty. One day he came along to her cottage with a gift of money to help her out. He pounded on the door but she didn't answer. He suspected that she was in and kept knocking, but when there was still no answer, he went away. She saw him leaving and the next Sunday in church said to him: "I would have answered the door, but I thought it was the man come to ask for the rent!" Dr. Spurgeon pointed out that a lot of Christians are like that: God comes to their lowly door with the eternal gift, and they think He has come to demand something — He's come for the rent, He wants ethical dues! This is one thing the gospel is not. There is no good news in ethics.

2) *The gospel is not a cluster of good ideas and great beliefs.* As it is not a way of living, so it is not a way of thinking or believing. High, marvellous concepts about God, man, life after death — they are not the gospel. The gospel is not "God is love": that's a fine metaphysical, philosophical, theological statement. But the gospel is: "God so loved...that He gave His only begotten Son that we might have eternal life". It is the good news of an historical act of God, not a metaphysical proposition about God. Likewise the gospel is not a philosophy of religion or a course in systematic or dogmatic theology.

3) *Again the gospel is not a social panacea, a prescription for making the world better.* Harry Truman once made the statement that his American foreign policy was based on the Sermon on the Mount, and J. C. Penny said that his chain stores did business on the principles of Sermon on the Mount. It may be unfair to suggest that neither Mr. Truman nor Mr. Penny had ever read the Sermon on the Mount, or if they had read it, they didn't understand it. But even if they were speaking the truth, the Sermon on the Mount is not the

gospel. And even if there was in the New Testament a prescription or a panacea for this world's economic and social ills, it would not be the gospel either. It is a mistake to talk of the gospel as being the answer for man's social political and economic problems. Not many years ago an evangelist went up and down the land with a banner which read "Christ is the answer". Well, Christ is not the answer in the sense that he provides solutions for all our questions and problems. There are many times when the fact of Christ and His gospel provides no answers, but raises disturbing questions.

4) The gospel is not the new and final religion. At last the perfect religion has appeared: the gospel. In all the religions of the world except Christianity, man's main interest has been to search for and to find God. This has been his religious quest, through his theology and ceremony and ritual, in all their complexity. But the New Testament tells us that the gospel is not man's search for God, but rather God's search for man. It was not man who by his religious genius and intentions bridged the chasm between himself and God, by building his high towers of Babel up to heaven. It was God who came down across the chasm in the Babe of Bethlehem. This is the gospel: "God so loved the world, that He gave His only begotten Son, that whosoever believeth in him should not perish, but have eternal life." "God was in Christ, reconciling the world to Himself." God came and identified with man in his sin and misery, and involved Himself for man's sake.

What I am saying is that the gospel is not good advice, not good opinions and beliefs, not good solutions and answers, not good theories about man's religious quest. It is, as we stated earlier, good news.

B

The New Testament is clear, I think, on what the gospel is.

20

l) It is good news about God, who came into the world for man's sake. This God, who is not a theological proposition or some kind of doctrinal statement, but who is personal Father love, acted on our behalf. He emptied Himself in the Incarnation, in Jesus Christ, and became man, and on the cross at Calvary poured out all that He had in love and self-giving, for our sake. This is the gospel. It is not only good news *from* God, it is good news *about* God: that He has come and revealed Himself and acted in Jesus Christ. Because He has done this, we see and appreciate, and the central note of the gospel is one of joy and gratitude: it is good news.

This really is why the Christian Church has come down across the centuries with songs and hymns and anthems. It is, at heart, a religion of joy and gratitude. Some years ago, one of the great theologians of Britain, Adolph Deissmann, was asked what he thought was the central note in the New Testament. He replied: "The central dominant note in the New Testament is the note of joy." Over and over again we hear it — from the angelic song at the birth of Christ, to Paul's letters, and right through to the *Book of Revelation:* "Rejoice in the Lord, and, again, I say rejoice!" The gospel is glad tidings, good news, that God is Father love, and has come into the world in Jesus Christ.

2) Therefore the gospel is good news about life, about salvation. The word "salvation" is an old-fashioned word which tends to turn people off. They say: "Why are you using theological jargon?" But every time we turn on our television, the advertisers are trying to save us from something — whether it is bad breath, body odour, tattle-tale gray wash or malnutrition. They're always trying to save us with their particular product. And our schools are out to save us from illiteracy and ignorance, our hospitals and medical schools want to save us from disease — and so on and on. There is, you see, nothing wrong with the word "salvation". In religion it means wholeness, spiritual health, personal integration.

Some years ago, the editor of the *Hibbert Journal*, L. P. Jacks, said that the more he read in the New Testament, the more he was convinced that the dominant note was that of immortality. Well, I think he should have used another word, meaning the same thing to him — the word "life". This is the dominant note in the New Testament. Salvation means life: it means wholeness and health and integration. Jesus said: "I am come that they might have life, and that they might have it more abundantly." The author of the fourth gospel wrote: "In Him was life, and the life was the light of men"; "These are written, that you might believe that Jesus is the Christ, the Son of God; and that believing you might have life"; "This is life eternal, that they might know thee, the only true God and Jesus Christ, whom thou hast sent".

Those terrifying words which we call "theological jargon" are mostly words which have to do with salvation or life. "Justification" means forgiveness for our past sins; "redemption" means liberation from our present sins; "sanctification" means new strength against future sins; "deliverance" means that we have been set free from sin (and egoism and fear and despair and futility and death); "reconciliation" means that we have been put right with God. These are words integral to the gospel. Can anyone say they are not good news? Do they not reach men and women, all men and women, at the very point of their deepest and most radical need — their need for "salvation", for "abundant life"?

3) *The gospel is good news about power.* By "power", I do not mean physical force or coercion, but spiritual power, energy and vitality, spiritual resources. One of the words which recurs often in the New Testament is the Greek word *dunamis*, from which we get our words "dynamite", "dynamo", "dynamic". The gospel is about dynamic and power.

For example, the gospel promises men and women the

power to become new people. St. John says "to them gave He power to become the sons of God". We see Peter changed into a rock from a vacillating failure. We see Mary Magdalene, the harlot, becoming a clean, saintly woman. We see Saul of Tarsus, the chief persecutor of the Church, becoming Paul, the greatest Apostle in history. We see Augustine, the profligate scholar, becoming Augustine, the most brilliant theologian of the faith since the apostolic age. These men did not become new men by exercises in self-improvement: there is nowhere in the New Testament where we are given guidance in self-improvement and self-efficiency so that we may become self-made men and women. What we are told is this: that we cannot change, but we can be changed. We cannot on our own become new men, but we can become new by being born again. Just as we did not make ourselves to be born in the first instance, neither can we make ourselves be re-born in the second instance. It is always an act of God. It is an act of His grace, and of His spiritual life-changing power.

And God gives us not only the power to become new people, but also the continuing power to cope with the trials, hardships, and temptations of daily living. We don't need more knowledge. You and I have enough knowledge, plenty of ethical understanding. We know what we should do, what is right and decent and just and true and honest. What we need is the power to do these things — spiritual resources — not more knowledge, but more grace. St. Paul tells us that he cried out to God once and twice and three times that God might remove from him his "thorn in the flesh", which was his physical disability. God did not remove the handicap, but said to St. Paul: "My grace is sufficient for you, and in your weakness my strength will be your power." Later St. Paul wrote: "Now I am content. I can be abased or I can abound,...I can do all things through Christ who is my strength." The gospel is good news about power, which can liberate and reinforce us.

4) *The gospel is good news of hope.* An American

writer tells the story of a mine cave-in down in West Virginia some years ago, similar, I suppose, to the mine explosion at Springhill in 1956. A number of miners were trapped deep in the coal-mine and running short of oxygen. A rescue crew was brought in to try and get oxygen to them, and eventually to dig them out to safety. As the rescue team came close to the cave-in, one of them heard what sounded like a tap. They listened and heard "tap", "tap", "tap" on the solid rock. One of the men recognized the tapping as Morse code, and read the words clearly: "Is there any hope?" This is the word raised by you and me and every human being, trapped in our own failures and problems, in our threefold human predicament of sin and suffering and death: "Is there any hope?" The gospel is good news that there is hope.

In 1849, the year of the great Gold Rush, all kinds of people flocked to what is now San Francisco, a rough, tough frontier town which had no churches. Among them was a Methodist minister by the name of William Taylor, who later became Bishop Taylor. He had no church on Sunday mornings, but he would take a barrel and roll it down to the corner where most of the men were carousing around; and then he would step up on top of the barrel and cry out: "What's the news?" Everybody would stop and gather round, and Mr. Taylor would say to them: "Thank God, my brothers, I have good news for you this morning!" And then he preached to them the gospel — the good news about God, about salvation, about spiritual power and about a "lively hope". That is "the glorious gospel of our blessed God, which has been committed to my trust" and to yours.

III

HOW CHRIST MEETS OUR DEEPEST NEEDS

A few weeks ago I was asked to address a gathering of church workers at St. Paul's Avenue Road Church on the subject "Christianity — who needs it?" The more I thought about the subject, the more firmly I became convinced that the answer is a very simple one: everybody needs it. And by "everybody" I mean just that: everybody — male and female, young and old, rich and poor, black and white, oriental and occidental — everybody needs it. No exceptions!

A word of explanation and definition. I don't think that everybody needs Christianity in some of its forms. Christianity as a philosophy or an ideology we can do without perhaps. Christianity as a particular religious organization or form of worship may be secondary. Christianity as ethics is not essential: every religious group has its golden rules, its commandments and its paths to purity. Nor does everybody need Christianity as doctrine: it is possible for men to believe the best doctrine, and yet be devils in heart and life.

What kind of Christianity am I talking about then, when I say that Christianity is needed by everybody? In our Wednesday evening study group we are dealing with a book by Professor Norman Pittenger, (a Professor of Theology at Cambridge University,) the title of which is *Life in Christ*. That is what I mean by being a Christian: Christianity in its essence means life being caught up in Christ. Phillips Brooks, the great Episcopal preacher of Boston, and later Bishop, was once asked by a student of Harvard

University if he felt that it was necessary for a Christian to have a personal relationship with Jesus Christ. Phillips Brooks answered, "My young man, that is what Christianity is all about!"

I wish that more of us would get that through our thick skulls! Christianity is not a simple ethic — paying our taxes, being decent to our neighbour, and keeping our nose clean morally. It is possible to do all these things and be a Buddhist, or a Confucist, or a Jew, or even an atheist. Christianity is something unique: it is our life being identified with Jesus Christ, so that His life is our life, and His will is our will, and His mind and purpose and heart become our mind and purpose and heart. (Doctrine, ethics, order and ritual are secondary.)

So we see that Christianity in this definition is not one among many religions, Christianity being suitable to us whites in the Western world, while other people in China, India, Africa and so on have their own religions suitable for them and do not really need Christianity. I do not believe that for a moment! Christianity is not one of a number of religions all equally good and suitable to their particular environment and culture: that is the ethnic heresy. Jesus did not put any limitations upon the validity and the universality of his type of religion when he said: "I shall draw all men to myself". All men. For Jesus was not a European, or a Westerner, or a white man; and Christianity did not begin around the North Atlantic, but in the Middle East. Christ is valid for everybody or for nobody!

This also means that Christianity is not just another interest or option, like folk-dancing, the opera, chess, golfing, carpentry — important only for those who have an interest in it. Christianity is a life and death matter. Listen to Jesus: "I am come that men may have life, and that they may have it in all its fullness." He meant life for every human being, not just for you and me. Likewise when he said: "I am the way, the truth and

26

the life."

Christ meets our deepest needs, and not ours only, but the deepest needs of all human beings. What then are these deepest needs? There are a number of them, and I'll hang them each about a certain man's name: remember the name and you will remember the need.

1) First, there is *our need for love*. We see this in children. Some children are starved for love. In our affluent society, where we are apt to construe the needs of children in terms of good food and shelter, the comforts and conveniences we can afford, a good education and a fine start for life, we should learn to recognize that their basic needs are actually very different from these. And the first of them is the need for love.

Great psychologists like Dr. Erich Fromm, Dr. Eric Berne and Dr. Muriel James are making much of this today, but the first of the great psychologists to do this was Sigmund Freud. It is rather unfortunate that Freud's name and the word "sex" are so closely associated. It is true that he focussed closely on the fact and the power of sex, in every human being, warning that a policy of hush-hush was not going to do anything to correct the problems and neuroses of people. But let us remember that when he used the terms "sexual" or "sexuality", Freud was using them as the Germans might well use the word "love", which refers to all of our affectional relationships — our love for children, parents, friends, neighbours within the community and the world, as well as for our spouses. Basically man is a relational being who cannot exist properly without love, understanding and compassion.

If this is true, it means two things: that we must be loved, and that we ourselves must love. On both these points Christianity meets this basic universal human need for love. When we turn to Jesus, we hear him say: "God so loved the world..." He talks about God as being the father of infinite love, whose love is for each and every one of us. We are loved.

27

God is not an impersonal force or principle that cannot see or know or hear. We are not just so many digits in the masses that have come and gone: we are individuals living in God's love. And so the Gospel of Christ says that we are loved; but it also adds that we must love as we are loved. "This is my Commandment," said Jesus, "that you love one another, as I have loved you."

2) One of Sigmund Freud's colleagues, Alfred Adler, broke with Freud because of what he considered to be Freud's over-emphasis on sex. Adler maintained that the great need of all human beings is not so much the need for love as *the need for significance or worth,* the need to be valued, (which he included under the concept of "the will to power"). The individual person needs to have a sense of his own value and significance. From early infancy on, all human beings have to overcome the feelings of helplessness, weakness and dependency which accompany infancy, in order to acquire a sense of personal worth, importance and uniqueness.

It is easy to appreciate Adler's emphasis on this need for a sense of personal worth and significance when you know people who lack it. They are neurotics, or timid people smitten with an inferiority complex, or loners trying to live and find their worth in a dreamworld of fantasy and make-believe — all of them constantly being frustrated by daily living. They need to listen to Jesus. If they will, they might hear Him say something like this:

One thing I want to do for you is to give you a new status — one that doesn't depend on a large salary or a fine address or whiteness of skin or anything like that. You are a child of God! Think of it! You are a child of the very Sovereign Creator of the whole universe. No other person, or state, or society, or government, or power-elite can take that from you. That is the very citadel and heart of your inalienable rights. Your dignity, your worth, your freedom, all belong to you, because you belong to God. You are His children!

28

When Jesus says that sort of thing, he enables us to hold up our heads. A true Christian can stand up to any power, any elite, any colour, in the knowledge that he is a child of God. Christians have been doing this all through the centuries, ever since the days of those lowly Galilean fishermen. "Not many wise men, not many mighty and not many noble" were called: rather, fishermen, peasants, tentmakers and slaves who had been given a new sense of personal dignity and worth. But with them God put to rout the V.I.P.'s the Ph.D.'s and the exalted Lords.

3) Another colleague of Sigmund Freud who broke with him on his over-emphasis on sex was Dr. Carl Jung. Jung contended that the deepest need in human beings is neither the will to power or significance, nor the need for love, but *the need for security*. There is something in us which craves for the security the infant feels in its mother's arms. Ever since infancy we have felt insecure. And so we tend to look to our great men — heroes who have stood up against demons and monsters and even the gods: and in these examples of power and courage we find some sort of security and hope. Well, be that as it may, we do know that many people have neurotic problems, and that all of us at some time or other are victims of fear and anxiety, because we are all basically insecure.

That is why every one of us needs Jesus. In Him and His Gospel and Resurrection there is a power and security which are of an ultimate, spiritual nature. How often in the New Testament there appears the little Greek word "dunamis" from which we get our words "dynamite" and "dynamic". "Dunamis" means "power": the early Christians had this power to live by, to overcome, to face the hardships and the demands of living — what Paul Tillich called "the courage to be". In the teeth of a cruel, totalitarian state they could say: "I am persuaded that neither death, nor life, nor angels, nor principalities, nor powers, nor things present, nor things to come...shall be able to separate us from the love of God, which

29

is in Christ Jesus our Lord." In the face of hostility and persecution, hardship and death they had inner security. Whether Jung's analysis is right or not, the need for security is surely met in Jesus.

4) A year ago this coming February (1973), Dr. Viktor Frankl, the great Austrian psychiatrist, spoke to three thousand people packed into Massey Hall. He declared that man's deepest need is neither the will to power, nor the need for security, nor the need for love, but *the need for meaning, personal meaning in his own life and existence.* True, we do need to know that there is meaning in the universe — that it isn't an accident caused by blind chance. And we do need to know that there is meaning in human life generally — that it isn't "comedy, or high tragedy or plain farce". But more than our need for a sense of meaning in the universe, and in human life generally, each of needs a strong sense of personal meaning. Dr. Frankl said we are living in a time of collective neuroses because of meaninglessness, and that this is at the root of the problem of the increasing suicide rate, the drug culture, crimes of violence and anarchy. That until individual human beings get a sense of their own personal meaning, life is empty, barren — it has no point. And if life has no point, why bother going with it? Why not lose yourself in drugs? Why not explode the "whole damn thing" and take it down with you in crimes and violence? Why not disrupt and destroy?

Turning to Jesus, we see that he spoke to men and women as if their lives had a basic meaning, not only as part of the nation or species, but as individual persons. In the sight of God their lives counted, and had a point. Jesus called fishermen like Andrew and Simon Peter his brother, John and James the sons of Zebedee, and he injected into their lives such meaning that they went forth with purpose, direction, motivation, and power, to live victoriously. He can take our little lives, and pick them out of their dull and wearisome slots,

30

and put them in a large framework which gives them point and meaning, by linking them to the purposes of God and His Kingdom.

5) In his book *Christianity and Psychology,* F. R. Barry points our another basic human need:

Few things so disintegrate our lives and so paralyse our effort for the future, as self-reproach and remorse about our past. And even where the sense of guilt is unwarranted, or an illusion, it is one of the most difficult things to cure.

In other words, what F. R. Barry is saying is that one of our basic needs *is the need for forgiveness.* Some psychologists never get around to talking about this. Some of them do, and one of the great psychologists, Dr. Hadfield, remarked that most of the patients who came to him didn't need a psychologist, they needed a penitent's-bench or a confessional. Their problems arose from unresolved guilt.

Conscience is universal. There has never been a race of people without conscience, without having a sense of right and wrong of some sort or other, without having to make up their minds on certain values and value-systems. Some things count more than other things, and eventually when men deny the things that count the most, they are smitten in their conscience and have a sense of guilt, which they themselves cannot dispel or resolve.

Man is a fallen creature. The Bible points this out. Let's not be fooled by "liberal" ideas that man is a reasonable, rational, kindly beneficent, well-disposed, peaceable creature, who will always do what is wise and good if not corrupted by society or economics, etc. That's only the fictitious "noble savage" of Jean-Jacques Rousseau's philosophy. No, man is a sinner with a conscience. He knows that he has disobeyed, that he has done the things he ought not to have done, that he has defied his own value-system, and even the value-system of the cosmos.

And so he must be forgiven. But he cannot forgive himself, for his sins have not been just against himself, but also against his fellow man, against the moral structure of the universe, and if he believes in a personal God of righteousness, against his God! What he needs, what every man needs, is divine forgiveness: the divine assurance that he is accepted and forgiven. What a release, what inner peace comes to a man's soul then! What a sense jof liberation and freedom! Christ meets that deep need. Listen to Him: "Neither do I condemn you. Go and sin no more;" "Father, forgive them..."

6) I believe that our most basic need, however, is not the need for forgiveness, or meaning, or security, or worth, or love, but *our need for God.* Since we are spiritual creatures, not animals or vegetables, but made in the likeness of God, He is our deepest and most basic need. You can hang this idea about the name of St. Augustine. He gave us this memorable statement: "O God, our hearts are restless 'til they find their rest in Thee." In other words, our lives are agitated, disturbed, empty, fragmented and unfulfilled until they find their fulfilment in God. The great American statesman, Adlai Stevenson, said the same thing: "man's most basic need is not for food or shelter or for the comforts of this world; man's most basic need is for God."

And is it any wonder, if we are spiritual beings, living souls made in God's likeness, that without Him we are just orphans? An orphan is a poor, pathetic, miserable creature — unless he finds another father and mother. And isn't that just what is happening with the spiritual orphans of our day? They are finding other fathers and mothers, fleeing to all kinds of idols and cults, because they cannot endure being perpetual orphans. But why run to second-best, or even cruel, foster-parents, when our True Father is waiting for us with open arms!

32

In Jesus we come face to face with God. This is why the early Christians called him "Emmanuel", meaning "God with us", and why they found no other title big enough for him but "Son of God". In him their deepest need was met, their need for the God who had created them. But "wonder of wonders", almost too good to be true, the God they met in Jesus was in His essence Father-love.

Who needs Christianity? Everybody does, because in its essence Christianity is "life in Christ" — life with love and significance, security and meaning, forgiveness and spiritual Sonship.

IV

THE GREATEST THING IN HUMAN NATURE

And the Lord God formed man out of the dust, and breathed into his nostrils the breath of life; and man became a living soul.

Genesis 2:7

When I consider the heavens, the work of thy fingers, the moon and the stars which thou hast ordained; what is man, that thou art mindful of him, and the son of man, that thou visitest him?

Psalm 8:3,4

In our time human nature is being seriously dehumanized by such great corporate evils as war, violence, racism, the denial of basic human rights to millions of people in countries such as the Philippines, South Korea, Brazil, Russia and other countries behind the Iron Curtain. But man is being dehumanized not only by such corporate evils, but also by such systems as have been created by modern technology, super-industrialism and urbanization — where human beings tend to become hands, numbers, functionaries in overalls, cogs in the great industrial machine.

Man is also being dehumanized by naturalistic and materialistic theories in Philosophy, Psychology and Sociology. For example, Edmund Wilson wrote a book called

A Piece of my Mind shortly before his death. (Edmund Wilson was the leading literary critic in the United States). In it he said: "Nor is it possible any longer to make the old-fashioned distinction between man and the lower animals, which enabled us to claim for ourselves something noble which we called 'the soul' which the other animals did not have." In *The Naked Ape,* Desmond Morris tells us that there are 193 different types of apes. 192 have hair all over their bodies. Only one ape, the human ape, has very little hair on his body. He is the naked ape. And somehow or other he has got exalted notions and calls himself *Homo sapiens,* "the wise one". In *African Genesis,* Robert Ardrey describes man as a vertebrate, a mammal, a primate, a hunting primate. He adds that if man imagines that he is unique or central or permanent in the natural world, he is seriously mistaken. There is no fundamental gulf between the world of the human, and the world of the plants and the animals. In other words, as another writer put it: "I see no reason for attributing to man a significance different in kind from that which belongs to a baboon or a grain of sand."

One wag wrote this little verse about human nature, about man:

> *First he was a tadpole, beginning to begin,*
> *Then he was a frog with his tail tucked in;*
> *Then he was a monkey in a coconut tree,*
> *And now he's a professor with his Ph. D.*

Somehow or other in our time, we need very seriously to recover what we might call the Christian Anthropology, the biblical view of human beings — this to be set over against the Marxist or the Freudian, or any naturalistic or materialistic anthropology. Not that we want a new debate on Genesis versus Geology, or a renewed quarrel between religion and science. But we do want the recognition that when scientists examine the human being, they must of necessity do so from a special or particular point of view: the physicist, from his point

35

of view, the chemist from his, the biologist from his, the economist from his, the psychologist from his, and so on and on. None of them studies the total man. None of them gets at the root or the essence of human nature. And therefore it behooves none of them to pontificate about man as a total being or person. Surely common sense makes it clear to us that there is a vast gulf between the world of plants and animals and the human world, which cannot be ignored or explained away, let alone be bridged. The greatest thing in human nature isn't anything we have in common with the plants or animals. It isn't our bodies. The horse, the dog, the peacock, the lark — all kinds of animals and birds — have certain bodily functions far beyond anything we possess. And yet we do not feel inferior to them as a species. Nor can we have a very profound or meaningful relationship with them.

What I am saying is this: according to the Bible and Christian theology, there is something distinctive and unique in human nature which differentiates a human being from every other creature in God's universe. Dr. Lynn Harold Hough, a very prominent minister some years ago in both the United States and Canada, in one of his books tells a story of a group of learned men who met together one evening to enjoy one another's company and conversation. The question was raised: "What is the greatest thing about a man?" One of them replied: "Why, of course, it is his ability to think!" "Not at all," said another, "It is his power to decide, his power of will!" "You are both wrong!" said the third man. "It is his power to feel! All the great things in life go back to man's emotions." Then a fourth man said: "None of you has gone far enough. The greatest thing about a man is his capacity to get into a moral fight!" (That is, to take seriously great ideas and values, and to enlist in great causes.) Well, what is the greatest thing in human nature? Let us look at the comments of these four scholars.

1) *Man's ability to think.* Man is *Homo sapiens,* the wise one, as we have said. He is far beyond the animals in intelligence, though the animals do possess rudimentary intelligence and intellectual capacities. One of the greatest philosophers of our century, Ernst Cassirer of Yale University, says that there is a clear distinction between the intelligence of the animals and the intelligence of the human. The animals do not possess symbolic imagination. They are unable to do relational thinking, reflective thinking, futuristic and purposive thinking, and abstract thinking such as we have in mathematics. Pascal, a philosopher of great distinction some centuries ago, wrote:

Man is a reed, But he is a thinking reed...If the universe were to crush him, man would still be more noble than that which killed him, because he knows that he dies, and the advantage which the universe has over him. The universe knows nothing of this. Our dignity consists in thought... By space the universe encompasses and swallows me up like an atom; by thought I comprehend the world.

Our ability to think is certainly part of our human greatness. Is it not then to our shame that we do not think? That we neglect our power of reflective thought, or relational thought, symbolical thought, abstract thought, philosophical and theological thought about great ideas and concepts? All of us most of the time, and many of us all the time, never really think. We re-shuffle our prejudices, or we muddle along in the old ways of habit and convention, or we "think" with our instincts and appetites, or we follow the crowd and copy the group and its mass-thinking, or we waste our brain-power on trivia and superficialities. No wonder a mathematician such as John D. Williams of the Rand Corporation was prompted to tell the National Council of Teachers of Mathematics in the U.S. that machines will become more intelligent than man. But he did give his case away when he urged the creators of intelligent artificial brains to strive for machines that are designed and built specially for abstract thinking. Note that the creators of these brains are not other machines but human minds. Creative thought, whether in machines or in a Sonata or a sonnet or philosophical system, comes only from men and women.

According to the New Testament, Jesus' first commandment requires us to "love the Lord our God with all our *mind...*" George Bernard Shaw once made the comment facetiously: "Most men never think. I think once a week and have become world-famous for it!" As we said earlier, most of us never do any real, profound reflective thinking on the great issues that confront us and our world. Today we are living in a critical age. It has become trite and hackneyed to refer to "the modern crisis". But surely man, with the glory of his capacity to think, should be able to confront our modern problems in depth and with reason, and with some perception for a solution. A modern artist had a cartoon in a local American paper. Two apes were looking at the ruins of a great city — everything destroyed, and nothing but the debris and rubble to be seen. No signs of life or survivors around anywhere. One ape said to the other: "You know, they say that these people were remarkably clever!" Yes, clever enough to invent the bombs that destroy but not intelligent enough to invent the techniques of peace and justice.

2) *Man's ability to decide.* This is his power of free will, the freedom that man has within his personality. This, of course, will be denied by the philosophical and theological determinists, and by the psychological behaviourists. They tell us that man, like the Skinnerian rat, is not free, but that everything he thinks, says and does is determined. Now surely, again, common sense tells us that this is hardly the truth, or else the poor behaviourist psychologist cannot be taken seriously because he's only *determined* to tell us that, and we are only

38

determined to believe or disbelieve it. This is a circle, going nowhere.

We do not mean that man behaves capriciously, with no cause behind his actions whatsoever: that he is totally and completely free, his own person. This is not true. The influence of heredity and environment upon us is profound. But we do insist that as human beings we are not things, or robots, or automata, and we are not animals acting by instinct, appetite and conditioned reflex. We are creatures who, at the very centre of our being, have the power to decide, to act with an element of freedom. It is this which makes us persons.

Isn't this, also, which is the basis of all innovation, and of all change? One of the distinctive marks of a human being is his ability to change himself — "the power to become", as Palmer, the psychologist, put it. Another is his ability to innovate changes in his environment. Another is his accountability and moral obligation: his power to decide. Are these not at the basis of our whole social order — that human beings are responsible, progressive and innovative individuals? In a democracy, and surely as Christians, we must believe that at some point we are free, responsible persons. This is part of our glory, even greater, perhaps, than our ability to think.

But is it not also part of our shame that we have the power to decide, the capacity of freedom to a degree, and yet neglect using it in socially constructive and ethical ways? We cannot opt out by attributing all our actions to our environment or our heredity, any more than to our stars or to our glands. We must acknowledge that we have failed to use our moral freedom in a mature and sensitive manner. This has been the sad story from the disobedience of Adam and Eve in the Garden of Eden, and the murder of Abel by his brother Cain, to the story of Noah and the Flood, and the arch crime of history, the crucifixion of Jesus and the responsibility of Judas, Caiaphas and Pontius Pilate. It has also been the story of our human race since those days: in Genghis Khan and

Napoleon Bonaparte, in Joseph Stalin and Adolf Hitler, in Richard Nixon and Jed Magruder, and in you and me! It is our shame that we decide for the sordid, the cheap, the mediocre, the destructive, the anti-social and the selfish!

But if we could not decide at all, and had no freedom to choose, we would, like the animals, be exempt from shame and blame. A cat can be taught not to kill chickens, but she cannot be taught why she should not kill them. A horse may kick his young owner and kill him, but he will not toss and turn all night with a bad conscience over it, or cry out to his Maker: "Have mercy upon me, O God, for I am a sinful horse"! Only human beings can accept blame and feel shame, because they alone have the ability to make value judgements and accept moral responsibility. And, as Rufus Jones, the great philosopher, once put it: "There is nothing more august in the world than to see a man step forward in a moral crisis and say: 'Here I stand. I cannot do otherwise. God help me. Amen.' "

3. *Man's ability to feel.* The third scholar said it isn't man's ability to think or his ability to decide, but rather his ability to feel that is his distinguishing characteristic. Man is not just a brain, or a brain plus a will. He is also an emotional creature. The ancient Greeks understood this and they classified the human emotions. The ancient Hebrews understood it, and in their religion they included all the emotions: joy, sorrow, laughter, pain, dejection, jubilation. Read the Psalms. And the stories of the prophets. In our Protestant, Calvinistic version of Christianity we tend to deal with man as if he were only a brain and a will. As a result, our Christianity often becomes rationalism, dogma, ethics and social responsibility in a cold or tepid and unattractive mix.

But our religion should never be just propositional and ethical, appealing only to men's minds and wills. It should also appeal to their emotional nature and drives; because men, in the last analysis, act not as much from their reason as from their emotions, not from their concepts as much as from their symbols. Jesus recognized this and used symbols in a powerful way in His teachings. He also declared that men's worst sins were the sins against feeling and caring and emotion: indifference, isolationism, lovelessness and pitilessness. People who did not care or feel could not be moved by the problems and sufferings of their fellowmen. On the other hand, the greatest virtues according to Jesus were love, sympathy, compassion, kindness and brotherhood. Therefore our religion should appeal to our feeling and involve the great emotional powers within our nature. We do not mean that our Christianity should be a thing of fanaticism, sentimentality and emotionalism, or our ethics soft-headed, irrational and unbalanced.

4. *Man's capacity to get into a moral fight.* This is a profound insight. Animals do not know what it means to be dissatisfied with their lot in life. They produce no reformers or prophets, protestors or dissenters, crusaders or wise statesmen. It is reserved for human beings alone to be moved by great ideals, values and causes. From them alone will rise up a prophet — a man totally dissatisfied with the status quo, or with some exploitation or injustice against his fellowmen, and who will opt for a better world, and hitch his wagon to a better star. Only among the humans do you get the Moseses, the Shaftesburys, the Kagawas and the Florence Nightingales.

Notice that when Jesus called His disciples, He did not call them merely to become pupils, or members of a new religious organization, but to become *followers* in a moral fight, the one for which He had been sent and to which He committed His life: to disperse the Kingdom of Darkness, the kingdom of evil and despair and death, and to inaugurate the new Kingdom of justice, liberation and human hope. Listen to Him: "If any man will come after me, let him deny himself, and take up his cross daily, and *follow* me." He was challenging men and women to enlist in a moral and spiritual struggle, and promising them a hard fight but an ultimate victory.

Of course this is both a unique capacity in our human nature, and the source of our failure and disgrace: that, being created to get into a moral fight, we have opted for neutrality, for personal ease, for our own self-interest and advancement; or, worse still, we have enlisted on the wrong side and thrown our energies and resources into the support of corruption, injustice, exploitation, racism and cruelty.

5) Somehow or other I feel that all four of these answers, good as they are, miss the real point. The greatest thing in human nature is none of these: man's ability to think or to decide or to feel or to get into a great moral fight. His greatest and most unique quality is *his capacity to have conversation and a relationship with his Creator.* It is this more than anything else which distinguishes the human animal from all other animals. Man has been called *Anthropos* — "the upward-looking one"; *Homo Religiosus* — "the religious man", who asks ultimate questions about the whence and the why and the whither of the universe, and himself; and *Homo Imago Dei* — "the God-like one", the very child of God, made in the image of God spiritually. And Plotinus referred to man as "The Great Amphibian". An amphibian is a creature, like a frog or toad, capable of living in two environments. It can live down in the dirt and slime of the pond, or it can come up and sit on a log in the sunshine and live there as well. It can exist in two environments. So man, by his very nature, can live in the physical worldly environment of getting and spending, eating and working, laughing and making love; and he can also live in a higher, invisible, spiritual environment of ultimate realities and eternal truths. He is never fulfilled living simply as a biological animal on the earth.

Philosophers talk of man's "reach for God" and his "search for the ultimate". Poets write about the human hunger for truth, thirst for reality and passion for the infinite.

Theologians like Augustine acknowledge to God: "Thou hast made us for Thyself, and our hearts are restless until they find their rest in Thee". Even statesmen and political scientists recognize that human beings are more than animals and slaves of the state, when they talk about men's "inalienable rights" — rights not conferred by nature or the government but by God Himself. As Martin Buber put it, man's essence is to have an I-Thou relationship with God his Maker. This is why man, alone among all God's creatures, prays, worships, erects altars and shrines, constructs chapels and cathedrals, expresses himself most profoundly through symbols, sacraments and rituals.

After her visit to the German concentration camps following the Second World War, the famous journalist Dorothy Thompson asked an old friend whom she found in Germany a simple question. He had served for twenty months in the dreadful death-house of Mauthausen, coming out of there half mummy and half man. The question she put to him was this: "Who behaved best among the inmates — business men? intellectuals? what race? what political parties?" The friend answered: "The priests". Miss Thompson commented later: "I shall remember that answer forever. They remained men in conditions of lowest bestiality who served an Image and an ideal higher than the highest achievement of men...in whom alone man attains significance and worth. They were those who knew that man as man is a soul."

V

A WORLD WITHOUT PAIN

For we know that the whole creation groaneth and travaileth in pain until now.

Romans 8:22

Body of twenty-year-old woman found in a field of goldenrod; police suspect foul play...Store owner shot by bandit...Stabbing case trial ordered...Falling scoop shovel kills Windsor man...Epidemic hits Saigon; 122 deaths already from cholera, about 2,000 expected...Automobile accident kills famous composer-playwright.

Items from Friday's newspaper

Now Friday's newspaper was just an average one. It contained no reports of terrific plane crashes, or dams bursting in Italy, or ships foundering in the North Atlantic, or earthquakes in Japan, and yet no day passes without its load of pain and suffering. "Man is born to trouble as the sparks fly upward." Pain is no respecter of persons — kings, scholars, and saints, are heirs to many of the same pains as slaves, savages, and scoundrels. Life for most of us has more happiness that pain, but for others, it contains more pain than happiness; and for nobody is it happy all the time. Ours is a world of pain.

We are all apt to cry out in protest, and like Thomas

Hobbes describe man's life as "nasty, brutish and short"; or like Oscar Wilde declare that there is enough suffering in any lane in London to deny the existence of God; or like the Persian poet Omar Khayyam, we may long to "break this scheme of things entire, and mould it nearer to the heart's desire"; or like an ex-missionary lady doctor, now retired in Victoria, B.C., flee from Christianity to atheism because of the troubles in this "vale of tears".

A minister tells the story of standing in a hospital room with the parents of a little girl who was in great pain. The best doctors had just told them that there was nothing they could do. The child's case was hopeless. The minister suggested that they pray together, the parents and himself, and the mother turned on him sharply and said: "You can't pray here to your God who lets a little child like this suffer. I wouldn't treat a dog that way."

This is a world of pain and suffering, and we are only trying to kid ourselves if we deny its ugly and distressing features, as the Christian Scientists seem to do, and call it all an illusion. A visit to a hospital ward, nursing home, slum or battlefield should put us straight. And it won't do any good to try and escape from this painful existence and become irrelevant and irresponsible like the Buddhists, in a world-denying religion, and dream about Nirvana. Nor will it help to turn to atheism and deny the existence of God. We then leave ourselves in complete darkness with no hope of meaning, and we compound the problem by raising a still greater question, of how to account for goodness, truth, beauty and love in a world without God.

There are still other false alternatives to which men and women have often resorted. There is the disposition to attribute everything to the will of God, like the Moslems who say, "It is the will of Allah." Some of us are more Moslem than Christian, and in the face of the most unnecessary tragedies and deaths, will say, "It is the will of God", or "God knows best, my dear". Such unthinking nonsense is an affront and a blasphemy against God. Then there is the tendency to say, "In the long run, things will work out right. We all get our equal share of trouble and pain, and our equal share of happiness and pleasure." But it isn't so. The facts deny it. Some people get much more than their share of pain and others much less. Nor is it true to say that trouble and suffering are the result of sin. The book of Job was written to contradict this doctrine of retribution. It is true that much of the suffering of the world is caused by man's sin, but not all of it by any means; and sometimes the best and noblest people are the greatest sufferers while the worst escape unscathed.

Nor is it very helpful to say that God is kindly disposed toward us but unable to help us. John Stuart Mill chose this way out: "Either God is good and not powerful, or powerful and not good." Mill preferred the first alternative. And so did H. G. Wells, in his own flippant way. Clarence Day, in *Life With Father*, says, "Any suffering that father ever had he attributed it solely to God. He never thought for a moment that God could mean him to suffer...His explanation seemed to be that God was clumsy, not to say muddle-headed." Such a point of view suggests that God is not God, but a feeble old ruler who has lost control of his realm, or a Frankenstein who has created a monster which he cannot handle.

What then? Well, today, I am proposing that what we do for a little while is to lift our eyes from the world of pain to a world without pain. Oh, somebody is jeering, and saying to himself, "Wouldn't you know it? The preacher wants us all to put on rose-coloured spectacles, so that the world's dirt and debris will look better. He wants us to live in a dream world, a 'Never, Never Land', a Shangri-la of comfort and bliss. His religion is like applying cosmetics to a corpse and then remarking 'How well he looks', or like sprinkling perfume around a sewer — just a camouflage or fraud." No, on the contrary, I want you to lift your eyes to a world without pain in order for you to see that it isn't heaven, but hell.

Aldous Huxley realized this truth, and in his *Brave New World*, gives us this picture: There is no effort any more and there are no tears. The savage, who has more sense than all the rest put together, looks at it, and nods his head and frowns, and says: "You've got rid of everything that's unpleasant. You neither suffer the slings and arrows or outrageous fortune nor take up arms against them. You just abolish them. And it's too easy. You need something with tears in it. Nothing costs enough here." A world without pain would be hell!

A

l) *Because in the first place, it would be a world without law.* Much of the pain and suffering of our world is caused by natural laws of the universe by which the world lives and functions. Things do not happen by chance, but according to the law of cause and effect. Given the same causes, with other factors remaining constant, you will get the same effects. This is inevitable in an orderly, rational, law-abiding system. Because of this, fire burns, water freezes, gravity operates day and night, and diseases kill. Even volcanoes and earthquakes, floods and pestilences are acts of law and not of chance.

Let us suppose that we could eliminate the possibility of suffering and tragedy caused by natural law. Then if a child drank poison he would not die. If an airplane's engine failed, thirty thousand feet up in the sky, it would not come crashing to the earth. If a ship sprang a leak and forced all its passengers and crew into the sea, no one would sink. Wouldn't that be a much better arrangement than our present system of law?

But we would have a crazy world, completely disorderly and unpredictable, where chance was king. Then our little child might die from drinking milk or eating blueberry pie — who could be sure of what would happen? If the law of gravity did not bring the airplane crashing down to earth, perhaps it would never bring it to the earth anymore. Airplanes might fall up, or away from the earth, and never be seen again, but be lost in space forever. If the people who were dumped into the sea did not sink, the sea wouldn't be fit for fish to live in, or for ships to sail in. We object when a brick falling straight down from a building under construction hits a man on the head and kills him. Let us suppose that bricks no longer fell straight down, but went flying off in all directions. Would we prefer a world of chaos and undependability, to an orderly and rational system? But to choose the latter leaves us vulnerable to pain and suffering caused by conflicts with an immutable universe. There are penalties as well as rewards, liabilities as well as assets, for living in a law-abiding world. And there is always the challenge to mankind to uncover the orderly laws of nature, and to learn to co-operate with them for the benefit of all.

2) *Secondly, a world without pain would be a world without human freedom.* Much of the suffering in world is caused because of man's free will. When God created man, He gave him free will, the power to choose between good and evil, right and wrong, truth and falsehood, and ever since, man has often abused his freedom and chosen the bad, and brought painful consequences upon himself and his race. The worst kinds of suffering come to human beings not because of the working of natural law, but because of man's inhumanity to his fellow man. This has been so from Cain to Herod, to Napoleon, to Hitler, to Adolf Eichmann, and from the wars of the cave men to the wars of the Persians, the Greeks, the Romans, to the global carnage of our own century. "Man's inhumanity to man makes countless millions mourn."

But this isn't fair. It isn't just. Why does God permit it? Why doesn't He make men do what He wants them to do? Surely He cannot be party to such injustices and cruelty? Why doesn't He prevent and stop wars, and blood baths, and political purges, and race persecution and tyranny?

What are we asking for? Do we want God to take from

human beings their power to inflict pain — their free will? The very source of their uniqueness and responsibility? In other words, do we want Him to turn us all into robots or automatons or puppets? To reduce our children to Teddy Bears or poodle dogs? That would of course diminish the amount of evil and suffering in the world, but it would also destroy the integrity and dignity of the human personality, lower the level of human living to that of instinct or machinery, and exclude the possibility of moral and spiritual greatness. No longer would it be possible for men and women to make a free and responsible choice for truth, purity or altruism.

3) *A world without pain would also be a world without human relationships.* We would have to live like Robinson Crusoe, alone on our desert island, where we could be quite secure and safe — until, alas, our man Friday appeared. As it is now, we live in a world of inter-relatedness, of inter-dependence, where human beings are bound together in the common bundle of life; a world "Where no man is an island, entire to himself, (but where) every man is a part of the continent, a part of the main"; a world where we are all members one of another, and where it isn't possible for any man to live unto himself or even to die unto himself. In this kind of world, if one man fails, he may bring tragedy on others; if one member of a family commits a terrible wrong, he may bring shame and disaster upon the whole household; if one politician or financier is corrupt or stupid, he may plunge a whole community or even a nation into trouble. None of us can live and act in a little isolation booth.

We may protest that it isn't right that the innocent suffer with the guilty, and even for them sometimes. It is a most unjust arrangement where our well-being and happiness depend on so many other people, where a few vain and truculent men can bring suffering upon millions of their fellow men in a global war. Would we be prepared to abolish all human relationships, and cut ourselves free from the

49

involvement of domestic, national, and racial connections, and go it alone? The alternative of isolation and independence doesn't look so good after all, does it? Our greatest values and treasures have come from our social inter-relatedness. Our knowledge, our language, our commerce, our inventions, our science, our philosophy, our music, our literature, our painting, our architecture, our friendships, and our religion, are all results of human inter-dependence. This becomes so evident when we think of our enormous debt to such benefactors as Moses, Plato, Shakespeare, Beethoven, Edison, Marconi, Lincoln, and above all Jesus. And our richest and warmest and most personal values are products of interdependence within the close-knit family — they are the fruits of human love. Would we renounce our heritage as "social animals" (to quote Aristotle) and exchange the whole mixed bundle of benefits and disadvantages for complete solitude? That is the only substitute for inter-relatedness — we can't have its benefits without its disadvantages. I don't think many of us would make that choice. Anyone who has endured enforced loneliness or abandonment or rejection knows that there is no worse kind of suffering that that possible for a human being.

B

There are also certain ugly derivative features in a world without law or freedom or inter-relatedness which need to be looked at.

a) *It would be a world without growth or progress.* As personalities, we only grow and develop because we have to encounter, and at least try to overcome, obstacles and hardships, and because we have to bear suffering and adversity. This also explains mankind's intellectual progress in the fields of research, inventions, and the social sciences. Problems of pain have challenged man's intellect and spirit, and called forth from him qualities that ease and comfort never demanded. Sir Julian Huxley, the famous British scientist, has put it in these words: "Without physical pain, there could be no adapted life and no progressive evolution. It is perhaps safe to say that there must always be pain of some kind if the human being is to advance from the infantile to the mature level of mind, from wish and fantasy and castles in Spain, to desire, tempered by experience, purpose, and real achievement." And Sir James Y. Simpson said the same thing in these words: "The successful species has come out of great tribulation." You see, "*No* pains, *no* gains." This is also the story of the Christian church — it has been the blood of the martyrs, and the ink of the theologians, which has been the seed of the Church.

b) *The second ugly derivative feature that I don't like is this: there would be no such thing as moral character.* You don't get character in a Teddy Bear or a puppet, or in an animal that behaves according to implanted natural instincts and has no free will or moral choice. Character is only possible where creatures are given moral freedom and responsibility, and are required to make decisions between truth and falsehood, right and wrong, good and evil. Only the free being can possess honour and integrity. He alone can climb the pinnacle of moral augustness, and declare: "Here I stand, I cannot do otherwise; so help me God."

And only the being that is bound in the bundle of pain and suffering can develop sympathy, one of mankind's tenderest and noblest qualities, and patience, and perseverance, and moral courage, and resoluteness, and generosity of soul. A world without pain would be a world without Buddha, Jeremiah, Francis of Assisi, Gandhi and Abe Lincoln. It would be a world without moral grandeur.

c) *And there is a third derivative feature which is just as serious. There would be no sacrifice.* The most glorious moments in human history are those when men and women have vicariously sacrificed their interests and comforts, and

51

even their lives, for the sake of their fellow men. Eliminate suffering and adversity and you would have no Socrates, no Father Damien, no John Huss, no Captain Oates, no David Livingstone, no Kagawa. And, what is much worse, you would have no Jesus Christ. No Calvary's cross. Would that be preferable to the world we live in now, where pain and suffering are not only possibilities but inevitabilities, but where God will take our suffering upon Himself, and suffer with us, and give us grace to overcome it and use it for beneficent and redemptive purposes?

Here is a poem which was written anonymously on the wall of a hospital room:

Lord, Take Away Pain

The cry of man's anguish went up to God,
  "Lord, take away pain!
The shadow that darkens the world Thou hast made;
  The close-coiling chain
That strangles the heart; the burden that weighs
  On the wings that should soar —
Lord, take away pain from the world Thou hast made
  That it love Thee the more!"

Then answered the Lord to the cry of the world,
  "Shall I take away pain,
And with it the power of the soul to endure,
  Made strong by the strain?
Shall I take away pity that knits heart to heart
  And sacrifice high?
Will you lose all you heroes that lift from the fire
  White brows to the sky?
Shall I take away love that redeems with a price
  And smiles at the loss?
Can ye spare from your lives that would cling unto mine
  The Christ on His Cross?"

We know that the whole creation has been groaning in travail together until now...and we know that in everything God works for good with those who love Him.

Romans 8:22,28. (R.S.V.)

VI

JUST AN ORDINARY JOE

(Isaac)

After I chose this title, it occurred to me that perhaps a better one might be the title of an old novel by Harold Bell Wright: *God and the Grocery Man.* In *Genesis 26,* beginning at the l8th verse, we come to these words:

And Isaac digged again the wells of water which they had digged in the days of his father Abraham, for the Philistines had choked them up.

I read a story some time ago about one woman asking another what sort of man her husband was. She got this reply: "Oh, just an ordinary type. 42 around the chest, 42 around the waist, 92 around the golf-course, and a nuisance around the house." "Just an ordinary type" — just the average man. Isaac was that kind of man. Abraham Lincoln said: "God must have loved the common people, for He made so many of them." There is no better example in the Bible of the average, ordinary Joe than Isaac. Isaac was a commonplace person sandwiched in between a noble, pioneering, great father Abraham, and a brilliant, flamboyant, unpredictable son Jacob. Abraham had blazed new trails, had dug new wells, and in his profound faith had established a covenant with God. But Isaac is remarkable for nothing of greatness. I looked up several books I have on Old Testament stories and characters: all of them dealt with Abraham, most of them with Jacob, but only a few with Isaac.

The story of Isaac is, as the title of a modern novel put it, *The Diary of a Nobody.* He was born, he grew up, he married, he tilled the fields, he had two boys, he ran their home, and he died.   Nothing spectacular, nothing exciting, nothing outstanding: no brilliance of intellect or spirit, and no brilliant exploration in politics and geography, like his father. Abraham was a great man; Isaac was an ordinary man.

A

Perhaps Isaac is an encouragement to us ordinary Joes and Janes. After all there are so few Abrahams, and Moseses, Isaiahs and Pauls, Luthers and Wesleys, Bonhoeffers and Niebuhrs: but there are so many Isaacs — in the pews and in the pulpits — parents and teachers, elders and preachers, Sunday School workers, and all the rest of us. And the Bible says that God was the God of Isaac: "The God of Abraham, Isaac and Jacob." Isaac must have been important as a link. Had he not been faithful to the profound faith and the new covenant of his father Abraham, Hebrew religious tradition would have ended there. But Isaac was faithful: he cherished the faith and the covenant, and preserved them for Jacob and future generations.

This is a real encouragement to us ordinary people. Abraham was a pioneer and an adventurous spirit, who left his parents and kin-folk in Ur of the Chaldees, and went to a far-away country where he began a new nation and a new religion. Isaac pioneered nothing and went nowhere, but he tilled the land and preserved the faith. Abraham blazed new trails, dug new wells, built new altars. Isaac brought nothing new into being, but he "opened again the wells of water which had been choked", and he walked in the paths that his father had blazed. Abraham commanded men, with authority and qualities of mind and spirit — a leader. Isaac commanded nobody, not even his wife, and his two sons Esau and Jacob. But he was a faithful husband and good father, who transmitted his religion

55

both by word and by deed.

There is a theory that the history of the world is really the biography of a few great men. Thomas Carlyle believed this. And Ralph Waldo Emerson agreed with Carlyle, and said: "Every institution is the lengthened shadow of one man, as the Reformation, of Luther; Methodism, of Wesley; Quakerism, of Fox...All history resolves itself very easily into the biography of a few stout and earnest persons." We cannot deny the great role that the Abrahams and Luthers, the Calvins and Augustines, the Platos and Pauls, played in directing and changing history. But surely the history of man and his world is not just the story of the battle of the giants, with all the masses of men and women being "the plurality of blockheads", as Carlyle called them.

Take the history of Christianity. St. Paul sets us straight here. It is not just the story of a few outstanding apostles such as Peter and himself. He says in *1 Corinthians 26:*

not many wise men after the flesh, not many mighty, not many noble, were called. *But God has chosen the foolish things of the world to confound the wise;...the weak things of the world to confound the things which are mighty.*

Isn't this what we discover when we read the Gospel stories about Jesus and his choice of disciples? He didn't comb Palestine to find special individuals, twelve important people — presidents of universities and lieutenant-governors; but ordinary men with rough callouses on their hands, the smell of fish on their clothes, and uncouth language on their lips. They were so ordinary that you cannot name six of them, without serious recollection. Read in *Romans 16* where St. Paul lists 35 disciples, such as Priscilla, Aquila, Hermas, Amplias, Urbane and Rufus — have you ever heard of them? 35 names of unknowns, anonymous disciples. And yet the Church marched forward to conquer the Empire and to move out into new worlds with these Nobodies, and not just with Peter and

James and Paul. The history of Christianity owes much to the Isaacs as well as to the Abrahams.

Isn't this also true of democracy? Why is it that we cherish it over aristocracy, oligarchy or monarchy? Because we believe that God can put to use the ordinary man and woman, and that the truth can come through the ordinary man and woman, and in the conflict of ideas of ordinary people we can govern ourselves. We don't need government to be imposed upon us by one superior person, or a small elite. We believe in democracy not because we think that every person is perfect and wise and rational and beneficent, but because we know that *nobody* is perfect and wise and rational and beneficent, and therefore no man is worthy to rule over us. In other words, the doctrine of original sin is one of the foundations for democracy.

Dr. T. R. Glover once said: "Democracy is clearly that form of government which asks the most from every citizen." That is right! It demands the most in wisdom, patience, goodness, character, moral courage and tolerance. The health and survival and real "success" of democracy do not depend upon one good and wise man, but upon each and every citizen. Democracy does not march forward only with the Gladstones and Churchills, the Washingtons and Jeffersons, the MacDonalds and Lauriers, but with the ordinary Joes, as well.

This is the reason why we read for our second lesson today Jesus' parable about the men with the talents. There were three of them and their master gave them talents in this order: one five, one two, one one. Let's forget the story and all its implications: that would require another sermon. But let us make one point: which one of the three men downgraded his talent, under-estimated it, buried it in the earth? The ordinary man, the man of one talent. Not the superior man of two talents. And not the genius of five talents. The greatest temptation is for those of us who are of ordinary capacities and gifts to underestimate them, and to reduce ourselves to

57

nonentities by burying them, as it were in the earth, where they can make no contribution at all to our country or to the Church of God.

B

From Isaac there are a few lessons we can learn.

1) The first one is this: that *an ordinary man can develop extraordinary qualities of character.* True genius is not genius of intellect but of character — of will and heart. "Knowledge is good, wisdom is better, but character is best of all." The greatest need of our world at the moment is not for more and better Rhodes scholars, inventors in science and research, pioneers in politics and economic production, but for more men and women of character; of goodness and compassion and kindness and a brotherly spirit. As John Oxenham, the British poet, wrote in 1917 during the days of the First World War, as they were predicting the end of the War and visualizing what would be needed in the postwar rehabilitation:

What we lack and surely need
For want of which we bleed, we bleed,
Is men of a more godly breed.

It is possible for an ordinary man to display extraordinary qualities of character.

2) *An ordinary man can serve God in a very ordinary vocation.* We make a serious mistake when we think there are only certain vocations suited to the service of God. For many centuries in the Church it was believed that there were two kinds of vocations: the religious and the secular. In the religious were priests, monks, nuns who were in the service of God. In the secular vocations were all the other workers who were in the service of the world. This belief was challenged by the Protestant Reformation. But there are still many of us who seem to think that there are special vocations reserved for the

58

service of God: we might broaden them to include teaching, medicine, nursing, and maybe another two or three. But we would not include business, labour, politics, engineering, law, architecture, and other mundane occupations. I wonder.

Years ago I read a little book called *Hiram Golf's Religion*. Hiram Golf was a simple man with plain virtues and a plain faith. He was a cobbler, and when he died the tombstone erected in the cemetery for him was a very plain one. But it bore the inscription: "Hiram Golf, Shoemaker, by the Grace of God." I could understand "Hiram Golf, Vicar, by the Grace of God," but "Shoemaker, by the Grace of God." Well that is Protestant insight into the nature of man's vocation.

I remember in my first congregation in Port Hawkesbury, Nova Scotia, when one day during the week just before Anniversary Sunday I saw a woman approaching the Church, carrying a pail and scrubbing-brush. I must have looked at her with some surprise, because she said to me: "You know, I can't play the organ, and I can't sing in the choir, and I can't teach in the Sunday School — but I can scrub!" And she scrubbed the floor of the Church for the Anniversary celebration, all the while humming old familiar hymn tunes. You don't need a round collar to serve God! Like Isaac, who tilled the land and tended the flocks and re-dug the wells, you can serve God in an ordinary, everyday vocation.

3) *An ordinary man can accomplish extraordinary deeds.* This is the history of Christian missions. William Carey was just an ordinary English Cobbler, but he took the Gospel to India. John Geddie was an ordinary Nova Scotia farmer, but he took the gospel to the South Pacific. Mary Slessor was an ordinary nurse, but she took the gospel to the West Coast of Africa. Walter T. Currie was an ordinary Canadian medical practitioner, but he took the Gospel to Angola. This is the history of the YM-YWCA: what was George Williams except an ordinary guy, a young Englishman who became concerned

that the youth of England were going to the dogs? One day he gathered eleven others whom he thought were also concerned, and together they formed the first little group of what eventually became the Young Men's Christian Association, now an International organization for the benefit of both sexes.

This is the story of prison reform with John Howard and Elizabeth Fry. They were not superior individuals except in character. And the story of evangelism: look at Dwight L. Moody, who shook America and Britain to their bootstrings — an ordinary Sunday School teacher who had been converted by another Sunday School teacher, neither of whom had even a high school education. Isn't this also the story of equal rights for blacks, and the tremendous movement for black liberation in the last fifteen years? It all began with a black woman by the name of Mrs. Rosa Parks of Montgomery, Alabama, who refused to be pushed around any longer and sparked the bus boycott. Even though the Isaacs are sandwiched in between the Abrahams and the Jacobs in all their brilliance and flamboyance, the contribution of the Isaacs can be incalculable.

4) *Another lesson: an ordinary man can make an extraordinary try.* The other day I read Margaret Truman's biography of her father, Harry Truman. About the time I was reading it Senator Barry Goldwater was quoted in the press on Harry Truman. As we all know, Goldwater is an arch-conservative among the Republicans, and Harry Truman was a liberal Democrat. But Goldwater said that Truman was the greatest President in America in this century. That ordinary man with only a high school education, greater than Woodrow Wilson who was President of Princeton University before he became President of his country? Greater than Herbert Hoover, the brilliant engineer and millionaire administrator? Greater than Franklin Delano Roosevelt with his New Deal and his charismatic personality? Greater than young John F.

Kennedy, the son of affluence and Harvard? Whether Goldwater's estimate is correct or not, you see it is possible for an ordinary man to make an extraordinary try. It was Teddy Roosevelt in his day who said: "After all, I'm only an average man, but, by Jove, I work harder at it than the average man!" That's the point. Even Thomas Edison, when asked to explain his genius, said it was 2% inspiration, and 98% perspiration.

5. *The ordinary man can draw on extraordinary resources.* He can tap the spiritual reservoir of power in the universe, and, through faith and commitment and prayer, become somehow or other linked to unlimited spiritual resources. He can be like an ordinary tree planted by the rivers of water, whose roots go down deep into the soil enabling it to bring the very forces of nature into the life of the tree. He can be like an ordinary battery which when attached to the generator of an automobile, receives new strength.

In *Luke 22* it is reported that as Jesus prayed in Gethsemane, *There appeared an angel unto him from heaven, strengthening him.* And what is true of Jesus has been true of other men and women who have taken prayer seriously. For prayer is, so to speak, "plugging in on God's circuit," and availing ourselves of the power which comes from Him alone.

Not a day passes but ordinary Joes and Janes, of no reputation or greatness, do great deeds, speak great words, overcome great suffering, and witness for Christ in very ordinary vocations. They do not accomplish great things simply by spitting on their hands, flexing their muscles, and mustering up unusual strength, but by letting God's power work through them.

And Isaac digged again the wells of water which they had digged in the days of his father Abraham.

Just an ordinary Joe!

VII

DAMAGED GOODNESS

Let not your good be evil spoken of
Romans 14:16

Catherine, the Smith's coloured maid, was talking
about another coloured woman who was quite a figure in the
community. "She's a sanctified saint in our church," Catherine
said. "I guess there never was a finer woman. She's good and
she's respectable, and she works for the church like everything.
But do you know what, Mr. Smith, she's got a hindrance. Even
her closest friends ain't fond of her."

Damaged goodness. Goodness with a flaw in it.
Goodness which doesn't commend itself to others. Goodness
which is less tolerable than badness. Goodness which instead
of being a label for Christianity is a libel against Christianity.
Let not your good be evil spoken of.

We must make it clear at the outset that St. Paul, in our
text, was not suggesting that his Christian brethren lower their
moral standards in order to win a cheap popularity. He did not
fear criticism or slander. He understood thoroughly Jesus'
admonition, "Beware when all men speak well of you." St.
Paul himself warned his people about selling out to the world,
about becoming conformed to the general pattern of human
behaviour, and throughout his ministry he endured more than
his share of calumny. The point he is making is simply this: a

Christian's goodness may falsify or caricature his religion and do Christ great harm. When goodness becomes a damaged article outsiders will be prone to say, "Well, if that's what Christianity means, we don't want any of it."

The question now arises, when is goodness a damaged article? I shall attempt to answer this with a brief treatment of five statements.

First, *Goodness is damaged when it is proud of itself.* That is, when righteousness becomes self-righteous; when we think that all is well in our moral life; that we are splendid examples for others to emulate; and that if only everybody was as good as we are all would be perfect in our community or nation. Clarence Day wrote of his father: "Father never once had any moments of feeling unworthy. He said he had no need to be better — he was all right as he was." The difference between Mr. Day Sr. and ourselves is more apt to be in his honesty than in our humility.

It is always a peril in the moral life that each conquest over evil will make us more satisfied with ourselves. As our greatest virtue, humility, arises from our sense of sin and unworthiness, so our greatest defect, self-righteousness, comes from our sense of goodness. That is the strange paradox of morality. The best illustration of it is Jesus' parable of the Pharisee and the publican at prayer. It was the sinful publican who was justified before God because of his humility, and the righteous Pharisee who was condemned because of his pride in his moral attainments. And was this not the trouble with many of the medieval monks and ascetics? They cultivated righteousness and then applauded themselves for it.

When we pride ourselves on our goodness, it is very likely that we are confusing sin with vice — adultery, drunkenness, theft and such palpable evils. But according to Jesus the worst sins are not of this type at all, but are sins of the spirit, such as envy, pride, selfishness, resentment and hatred. George Santayana has properly interpreted Jesus' reference to the harlots being closer to the Kingdom of God than the Pharisees in his remark, "It is easier to make a saint out of a libertine than a prig." Both Augustine and Francis of Assisi are illustrations of this truth.

Furthermore, self-righteousness inevitably leads to censoriousness. It sits in judgment over others, as the Pharisees over the adulteress woman, forgetting that we are all sinners in the eyes of God, and that only God can compute our comparative merits. John Milton once wrote that "A good man is the finest fruit earth holds up to God." It is true. But when the good man himself begins to admire or commend his own goodness he becomes the unloveliest specimen of human striving.

Secondly, *Goodness is damaged when it is mainly negative.* Most of us as youngsters were admonished to follow the example of the three wooden monkeys, who see no evil, hear no evil and speak no evil. Alas, much morality doesn't get far beyond that elementary monkey stage. It is a list of negations and prohibitions. Even such a writer as Thomas a Kempis suggests that the virtuous life can be achieved by getting rid of one sin after another, as though the abundant life morally consisted in eradicating an abundance of sins.

That was the historic error in much Hebrew ethics. The emphasis was altogether too predominantly "Thou shalt not". By the time Jesus was born the pharisaic laws numbered six hundred and thirteen and included three hundred and sixty five restrictions. A man was good if he refrained from doing so many wrong things. The fact that he may not have had any positive and radiant virtue was largely overlooked. It was enough that he was not a transgressor.

In Jesus' teachings there was a radically different emphasis. To Him goodness was positive in character. He summed up the law and the prophets in one great commandment: *Thou shalt love the Lord thy God...and thy neighbour as thyself.* He took the Golden Rule, which had been stated by moralists of many cultures, (Confucius, Hillel, eg.) but always in a negative form, and gave it a new force by making it positive, *Whatsoever you would that men should do to you, do you even so to them.* And in the parable of the Good Samaritan, the priest and the Levite were condemned because they did nothing, they lacked positive goodness. It will be so in the final judgement too, said Jesus, for those who will be cast into outer darkness will be those who have committed the sins of omission. It will then be clear how faulty and damaged an article negative virtue really is. If we are going to demonstrate Christian living in our time we shall never do it by an anemic and pollyanna or forbidden-fruit kind of goodness.

Thirdly, *Goodness is damaged when it is strained.* That is, when it is a sweaty, unnatural, effortful performance. There are people who misinterpret St. Paul's words to "work out your own salvation" and set themselves to the joyless task of achieving goodness by superhuman effort and salvation by works of righteousness. They do not understand that true moral growth, like physical stature, does not come by anxious thought and strain. but by an inward surrender and receptivity to the grace of God.

Betty MacDonald, in the *Egg and I*, has a character, Mrs. Hicks, who illustrates what I am trying to say. "Mrs. Hicks was good and she worked at it like a profession...I was surprised when I learned that Mrs. Hicks had a mother — she was so pure I thought she had come to life out of the house-dress section of Sears, Roebuck catalogue."

In his famous book *Ecce Homo*, Sir John R. Seeley pointed out that Jesus never lived up to His teachings — He lived them. What a splendid distinction. Jesus' goodness did not smell of perspiration. It came logically and easily from a great resource within His soul, and as the effortless beauty of the lily surpasses the effortful beauty of Solomon, so the beauty of Christ's goodness surpasses that of all the perfectionists and ascetics. They tried too hard; He was good without trying — if I may put it that way. They succeeded in pounding out a counterfeit virtue, He produced the genuine article. Theirs was a manufactured little thing tainted with body odour, His was a pure living fruit with a rich fragrance.

During a civic celebration in a small Western Canadian town the local band was playing "God Save the King". When all the other instruments were silent, the drummer added a tremendous beat on his drum. "The trouble was," he explained to the band leader, "I was watching the music too close and played a fly speck." That can happen with the moral drudge too, and his strenuous toil can destroy the beauty of holiness.

Fourthly, *Goodness is damaged when it is served in a pint measure.* Then it becomes the mere performance of defined duty and not the expression of divine grace. There is something lacking in goodness that never rises above the obligation imposed on us. It is a legalistic, rigid and stingy thing.

Again the Pharisees represented this kind of damaged morality. They were faithful to duty, but never went beyond the call of duty. They were faithfull to the letter of the law but didn't understand that real goodness doesn't appear until the law has been transcended. And so Jesus said to His disciples, *Except your righteousness exceed the righteousness of the Scribes and the Pharisees, you can in no case enter into the Kingdom of heaven.*

Christian morality is quite a larger thing than the pharisaic observance of law or the Greeks' practice of moderation. It is an extravagant eclipse of the demands of law and reason and duty, and never calculated less or more — something which overflows and outruns reasonable expectations and legal contracts. Else, "What do you more than others?" Others will go the one mile demanded, but you should go two miles. Others will forgive a man once, thrice, or even seven times, but you should forgive him seventy times seven. Others will obey the call of duty but you should take up your cross and follow One who was excessive in His goodness and went away beyond the call of duty.

I think it is clear why Jesus seemed to prefer the company of sinners to that of the "Saints" of His day. The "saints" were dutiful, calculating and cautious. The sinners were not only indulgent in badness, but they had their moments when they were indulgent in goodness. People of excesses like that are not only more interesting than niggardly souls but they are actually more lovable. And there is more hope for such scamps than for their "betters". What a warning this should be to those of us within the Church, professionally religious and professedly righteous. The prodigal wastrels are to be preferred to the unbending and obedient elder brothers.

Finally, *Goodness is damaged when it casts a chill.* Like the purity of the iceberg, it may be admirable but it is not companionable. When the Pharisees entered a room the temperature suddenly went down and everyone began to shiver, but when Jesus entered a room the temperature went up — His goodness radiated warmth, and the common people heard Him gladly. *The law was given by Moses but grace and truth came by Jesus Christ.*

Some years ago, R. E. Knowles wrote in the *Toronto Daily Star:* "As a boy, I thought of saints as pale people with feeble digestion, who stood apart and communed with Heaven and wished they were not alive." There was none of that kind of sainthood about Jesus. He loved life and people and goodness because he loved God, and there was a warmth and contagion about his goodness which was unique.

This does not mean that Jesus condoned sin and made feeble excuses for people's immorality. It means rather that His deeper understanding of human nature moved Him to a compassion which the strict moralists did not possess or even understand. They were quick to criticize Him as "the friend of sinners" — which He was, because He was ambitious for their redemption. He saw them as sick people who needed to be made well. They could be helped only by intelligent and loving concern, and not by cold and rigorous condemnation. While the Pharisees drove them further away from the Kingdom of God, Jesus drew many of them into a new life of purity and grace. His was the approach of the Prodigal's father instead of that of the elder brother. And down the centuries His love has been changing lives which could never be touched by the chilly keepers of the rules and conventions of morality.

In Jesus Christ we have the challenge of Divine Goodness. In Him we have the only valid motive for morality — we are to be good because God is good. And in Him we have the grace which can make us "more than conquerors". Apart from His spirit we can do nothing, and even our best achievements in virtue will be soiled and ragged works of our human frailty.

VIII

GOODNESS WITHOUT GOD

Sometime ago I happened to be at home one morning and listened to the CBC's radio program *Court of Opinion*. At the conclusion the four panelists were asked to suggest what they thought to be history's greatest quotation. The four replies were as follows: "Think" (IBM's famous motto), "To thine own self be true" (from Shakespeare's *Hamlet*), "No man is an island" (from John Donne's *Spiritual Meditations*), and "Love thy neighbour as thyself" (Jesus' words in a quote from the Book of Leviticus). We must make allowance for the fact that the panelists did not have much time for consideration. And we must agree that all four statements are significant ones, two of them great ones. But we must also be reminded that they are each and all inadequate and incomplete by themselves.

The first one, "Think", for example, is plain rationalism. You would suppose that a human being is just, or primarily, a brain, an intellectual machine to be sharpened and informed. This was the error of the Greeks, and the Rationalists, and is the error of the Scientific Humanists: that if human beings only know what is right they will naturally do it. The prophets of Israel knew better than that. They knew that man's real trouble was not in his brain, his ignorance and lack of education, but in his ego, his self, his spirit, which blinds his reason or overrules it by self-interest. St. Paul knew that there was a power working in his members contrary to both his reason and his will. Listen to this confession. "The good that I would I do not: but the evil which I would not, that I do." And surely we know that educated men are still sinful men, and enlightened civilizations are still threatened with egoistic and dark elements within. We are not going to be saved without thinking, but neither are we going to be saved by thinking. Just as the alcoholics' problem is not ignorance of the dangers of drinking, and the white racists' problem is not ignorance of the Negro's biological and spiritual equality, so our universal human problem is not illiteracy, misinformation, and unscientific thinking.

Or consider the second quotation, "To thine own self be true." This is plain humanism. It suggests that man's chief duty is to be true to himself, that there is no higher reference or obligation than himself, and that if every man would be true to himself all would work swimmingly in our world. Carried to a low extreme this doctrine leads to laissez-faire individualism and libertinism — a do-as-you-please philosophy, and an egoistic expression on one's self-love. But even when it is carried to a high extreme it sets each man up as the arbiter of his own case, and denies any obligation either to man or God, and is bound to lead to moral anarchy and disintegration, and the clash of millions of egos or little tin-gods.

The third quotation, by itself, is humanism with a collective rather than laissez-faire emphasis: "No man is an island." It stresses man's natural interdependence, and the basic needs for mutuality, co-operation, and goodwill. And we desperately need to learn these things in our day of nuclear weapons, satellites, space ships, and intercontinental ballistic missiles. Certainly "No man can live unto himself, and no man can die unto himself," "We are all members one of another." There are no "Isolation Booths", and there is "No Place to Hide". Science and economics know these truths; politics and social relations are gradually learning them the hard way; and religion has known them since the days of the prophets and

70

Jesus and St. Paul. But religion also knows this, that man's basic and most important relationship is not that with his fellowmen, in this interdependent bundle of life, but that with his Creator. No exhortations to brotherhood and altruism are adequate without a sense of God, in Whom we all live, and to Whom we all are of eternal worth, and before Whom we all are responsible as our brother's keeper.

Even the fourth quotation, "Love thy neighbour as thyself," is just Moralism. Of course it would be a wonderful world if every one of us loved our neighbour; that is, treated him as a person and not a thing; respected him for what he is in the sight of God; offered to him our goodwill, generosity and kindness; regarded him as our true brother. But this commandment to love our neighbour is incomplete in itself. Why should I love my neighbour? Is it because every man is really loveable when you get to know him? That's nonsense. Is it because every man will respond to love, and love will bring out his best qualities? That is not necessarily true. Is it because it is good for ourselves to love others? That is a selfish reason for an altruistic attitude — in other words, our altruism is really egoism, and we are using other people as means for our own ends. Is it because loving others will make for a better world? If so, then they are not to be loved for their own sake but for the sake of the whole. Again, that is not true love.

At this point I wish to quote Jesus. *Thou shalt love the Lord thy God, with all thy heart and soul and mind and strength. This is the first and great commandment. And the second is like unto it, Thou shalt love thy neighbour as thyself.* Jesus never separated the two — neither one is complete in itself. Love for our neighbour is the logical expression and practical test of our love for God. Nor did Jesus ever reverse the order of these two obligations: Love for God always takes priority, because God is God, and not just another human being, and because He is our Creator, and Provider, our Judge and our Saviour.

71

To hear even some of our most literate laymen speak these days one would think that they had never read the New Testament, heard of the works of the great theologians such as Augustine, Luther and Calvin, or even of such modern writers as Reinhold Niebuhr, Paul Tillich and C. S. Lewis. Moralism remains the laymen's prevailing "Theology", and they tend to regard the Christian faith as either a means of self-improvement, or a philosophy of social betterment, or both. If they would turn seriously to the New Testament they would note that the Gospel is God-centered and not man-centered; that the Christian's primary responsibility is not to himself or to his neighbour, but to God. It is only when we acquire a new relationship with God — one of love and trust — that we can acquire a new relationship with our fellowmen and truly love and serve their highest good. And of course it is only God who answers the ultimate questions of man's life — its meaning, purpose and dignity; and it is only God who can enable spiritual beings to find fulfillment.

It is a serious mistake to divorce morality and religion, ethics and theology, and think that morality can exist independent of religion, and is the more important of the two, in fact the only one that really matters. It is a common heresy to belittle religion, talk patronizingly about the Church, and debunk theology and doctrine, as so much mumbo-jumbo. As a matter of fact, Goodness without God is pretty inept and insecure.

For one thing, *it has no ultimate justification or support.* Without God it has no eternal validity, and carries no ultimate authority. It is an accident in an amoral universe which has nothing to which it corresponds. There then is no conscience or moral imperative, just our human desires and preferences.

In one of John Galworthy's stories Dinny says: "I don't see the connection between beliefs and character. I'm not going to behave any worse because I cease to believe in Providence or in an after life...If I'm decent it's because decency's the decent thing..." The Mother hits the nail on the head in her reply: "Yes, but why is decency the decent thing if there is no God?"

Even Jean-Paul Sartre, the French existentialist philosopher and atheist, agrees that if there is no God there can be no moral values, because we are on a plane where only men exist. He likes to quote Dostoievsky who said, "If there is no God, then everything is allowed."

Moral values are the fruits of theology. Because God is good we should be good. Because God is just we should be just. Because God loves our fellowmen we should love them. And if we truly love this God and Father of us all we shall come to love our neighbour too.

Secondly, *Goodness without God leaves us to act as arbiter in our own moral life.* Take the Golden Rule for example: *Do unto others as you would have them do unto you.* Who is to be the judge of what you do to your fellowmen? You are. Clarence Day, in *God and My Father,* says that "Whatever he [his father] did unto others he was sure was alright." Most of us are like Mr. Day, Senior, and feel sure that if everybody in the nation, or in the world, behaved towards others as we do, Utopia would be at our door. We are pretty smug about how we treat our neighbours, how well we provide for the poor, how generous we are in our dealings with other countries, and how fair are our trade and immigration policies. It is incredible how blind and complacent self-interest can make us.

This is why no Golden Rule is good enough without God, and no admonition to love our neighbour as ourselves is adequate apart from our love of God. George Bernard Shaw made this clear in his inimitable way when he said, "Don't always do unto others as you would have others do unto you. Their tastes might be different." A drug addict, a political schemer, or a woman-chaser would all judge their neighbour's good by different tastes and standards. Taken out of a theological context, you see, the Golden Rule is not even ethical, and could be downright immoral. As Paul Scherer put it, "Without the Gospel in front of it, it is nothing but an imperative without any visible means of support. The imperative must have its indicative. *God so loved the world*: therefore, *thou shalt love the Lord thy God, and thy neighbour as thyself.*

Thirdly, *goodness without God has no spiritual resources or dynamic behind it* — it is weak and impotent and generally peters out before long. George Santayana, the great philosopher, admitted that rational morality could only stand against a small temptation, not a big one; and so could only attain a small degree of virtue and not a large one; and only make a small sacrifice of self and not a costly one. This is why the ethical culturists and practical humanists never produce any Father Damiens or St. Francises or Jesus Christs. Goodwill needs a great and profound faith behind it if it is to become effective, or redemptive, goodwill.

Fourthly, *goodness without God offers no salvation.* It is so coldly impersonal and spiritually impotent. We can't ask forgiveness from the Golden Rule or The Ten Commandments or Confucius' maxims. We must either make light of our moral failures or carry our guilt without hope of relief. And then when we succeed there is no safeguard against our becoming smug and self-righteous. In other words, moralism fails us both at the point of our failures and at the point of our successes. It has nothing either for a great sinner like Mary Magdalene or for a great saint like John Bunyan.

Finally, *goodness without God has no destiny, no real goal of hope.* Its kingdoms are all of this world, in the form of earthly utopias or brave new worlds into which only those who can enter happen to reap the fruits of the many centuries of moral effort. But the whole scheme of things in the end adds up to nothing, has no ultimate destiny, because there is no God, no ultimate purpose and meaning. And so, when it is all said and done it doesn't really matter, not really, not permanently, not finally, whether we have been true to our highest self or not, or whether we have loved our neighbour, and given our best in mutual co-operation and good will. The last word is "Exit".

For Christians, the supreme, and perfect, example of goodness is Jesus on His Cross. In His death, as in all His teachings, His rule was obedience to God's will — which was love for God and for all God's children. Jesus never taught an ethic of idealism, or humanitarianism. He had no doctrine of virtue, or of doing good for goodness' sake. He gave no lectures on character building, personality values, the self-realization of humanity, social progress and development. For Him goodness consisted in doing the will of God: we should be truthful because God is truth, we should be just because God is just, we should be kind because God is kind, we should forgive because God forgives us, we should love because God loves us. "Like Father, like Son", was to be our only rule. *As* God our Father loved us, *so* we his children should love Him, and all the other members of His family, our brothers and sisters. There was no lecture on love "as a virtue which belongs to the perfection of man, or as an aid to the well-being of society." Just this: love God and this will determine your attitude toward your neighbour; love your neighbour and this will prove your love of God.

There we have goodness which has a likeness and support at the heart of the universe, goodness which is effectve, and goodness which belongs to a kingdom of Love and Victory: Goodness with God!

IX

THE MEANING OF THE CROSS

God commends His love toward us, in that while we were yet sinners Christ died for us.

Romans 5:8

There has perhaps been more heavyweight theological discussion upon the meaning of the Cross than upon any other subject in the whole field of our Christian faith. Theologians since St. Paul's day have wrestled with this "Mystery", and none has ever presumed to have penetrated its depths. Hence this sermon at best is but a modest attempt to say something relevant, not something adequate.

Why is it necessary for us to say anything at all? Because the Cross of Jesus Christ has had a meaning in history such as no other Cross has ever had — a glorious, and unique meaning, which we clothe in such terms as Atonement, Reconciliation, Salvation, Redemption, Deliverance. That meaning alone can account for the transformation of that cruel, cursed and contemptible device of pain and disgrace into an object of devotion, beauty, and power; for the blackest of all days being cherished by nineteen centuries as "Good Friday"; for the sign of the Cross becoming the sign of hope, and courage, and love for millions of human souls; and for the rapture of poets and preachers, artists and architects, mystics and musicians over that rough-hewn beam. That meaning alone can justify the early Christians going forth over land and

76

sea, across the Graeco-Roman world, where the Cross was an offence and a stumbling-block, displaying one symbol and proclaiming one theme, "the Cross of our Lord Jesus Christ".

What then was it that happened up there on Calvary that day? We use the term "Atonement" — what do we mean? Simply what the word says, at-one-ment — man and God are brought together into a oneness of relationship. Or we use the term "Reconciliation". This too means exactly what the word indicates — man and God are reconciled, a harmony has been achieved. Or we use the terms "Redemption", "Salvation", and "Deliverance". To be redeemed, saved or delivered means to be reclaimed or rescued or liberated — that is, to be set free from some tyranny or bondage. In Christian language that means to be set free from the power of sin and self, and saved for the "glorious liberty of the children of God".

Redemption does not mean that the past is all undone or that the consequences of our sin are wiped out. A man's sinful past can no more be undone than Judas Iscariot's repentance could undo the Crucifixion.

> *The Moving Finger writes; and having writ,*
> *Moves on: nor all your Piety nor Wit*
> *Shall lure it back to cancel half a line,*
> *Nor all your Tears wash out a word of it.*

Redemption does not put our past acts right. It puts our sinful selves right — our attitudes, ambitions, aspirations, and affections. It breaks the hold of sin upon us, thereby setting us free to good. It breaks the hold of self upon us, thereby setting us free from self-will, self-assertion, and self-sufficiency, to the joy and fellowship of the service of God. It works for us "an eternal weight of glory" which is best called "Salvation", and which can only be understood by those who experience its grandeur within the soul. Then do we cry out with the Apostle Paul, "God forbid that I should glory, save in the Cross of our Lord Jesus Christ."

Now we come to the question of how Christ effected this precious work of Salvation or Redemption. What happened to give His Cross its supreme meaning? Let me attempt an answer under four headings: 1) The Cross revealed the nature and heart of God; 2) The Cross revealed the worth of the Human Soul to God; 3) The Cross revealed the heinousness of Human Sin; and 4) The Cross released in the world the Power of New Affection.

First, *The Cross revealed the nature and heart of God.* Notwithstanding the revelation of God in the physical world, in history, in noble men and women, in Hebrew prophets and Greek philosophers, in mystics, seers and saints of all ages and races, never had He revealed Himself in all His Fatherly goodness and love as in the life and teachings of Jesus Christ — in His person, parables, pity and passion. And that revelation reached its climax at Calvary in the display of a love which would go to any lengths for mankind's sake; which would voluntarily subject itself to humiliation, weakness, suffering, and death, for the sake of those vile creatures which cast it out, made cheap mockery of it, and sought to take away its life. Such a pure self-forgetful, and sacrificial love could not but be the most Divine thing this world has ever looked upon. It is incomprehensible that the nature and heart of God are other than that. If ever God has been disclosed before men's eyes it has been at Calvary.

Diderot used to say to people of his day, "enlarge your God." That is the first thing which the Cross of Christ does for us. It enlarges our God, our conception of God, until He becomes a God without limits or dimensions, a God of infinite love. And that is the first work we all need done for us before we can know the glory of Salvation. We must be made confident of the depth and splendour of the mercy of God, His love must be commended to us as the unfailing love of a Heavenly Father, before ever we shall desire Him above our chief joy, and aspire to His fellowship and Service — that is,
78

before ever we shall desire Salvation.

Stanley Jones somewhere tells about a young child who burst out, after being taught about Jesus saving us from the wrath of God, "I love Jesus, but I hate God!" I fear that much of our preaching throughout the Centuries has denied rather than proclaimed the revelation of God in the Cross. And I submit that such preaching has done more damage to Christianity than all the burnings of the Inquisition. Because it denies the Christian gospel at its very centre — *God so loved the world that He gave His only Begotten Son,* and that *God was in Christ reconciling the world unto Himself.* Any theory of Redemption which paints God as an angry, hostile, proud Being, jealous for His affronted dignity, and insisting that His wrath can only be placated by the payment of the price of innocent blood, is a crude and blasphemous contradiction of the Gospel of the Cross. William Blake characterized the preaching of his day in this fashion: "First God the Father fetches us a clout on the head, then Christ brings us balm for our wounds." What we must see is that the whole initiative in the work of Redemption was with God, and that "the Cross of wood on which Jesus was nailed is the symbol of an eternal Cross in the heart of God."

In his fine book *Our Eternal Contemporary,* Walter Marshall Horton tells about a young woman brought by ambulance to a hospital, after having been stabbed in a drunken brawl in a disreputable quarter of an American city. The case was hopeless, and a nurse was asked to sit by the unconscious girl until death came. As she sat there looking in pity at that young face with such coarse lines upon it, the girl opened her eyes. "I want you to tell me something, and tell me straight," she said. "Do you think God cares about people like me? Do you think He could forgive anyone as bad as me?" The nurse did not dare to answer at first, until she had reached out to God for a kind of authorization, and reached out toward the poor girl, until she felt one with her. Then she said, "I'm telling

79

you straight: God cares about you, and He forgives you." The girl gave a little sigh, and slipped back into unconsciousness, the lines on her face changing to smoothness as death quietly overtook her.

The message of the Cross is that *God commends His love toward us, in that while we were yet sinners Christ died for us.*

Secondly, *The Cross revealed the worth of the Human Soul to God.* It placed a new valuation tag upon human beings. If they are worth so much that Jesus of Nazareth would go to His death on a Roman Cross for their sake, never again can they be thought of as cheap or common or contemptible. And once a man sees himself in the light of Calvary's estimate, he can be satisfied with nothing less than Redemption, both for himself and for his fellowmen — nothing less than to be reclaimed from a life of sin and selfishness and futility, and saved for (or to) a life of spiritual grandeur and high destiny.

Henry Sloane Coffin told a story about a French scholar of the seventeenth century, Muretus, who fell seriously ill in Lombardy, and was taken to a pauper hospital. There he overheard the physicians, who were consulting about him, say in Latin, not thinking that the poor sufferer could understand this language of the learned, "Let us try an experiment with this worthless creature." And from his bed the sick scholar startled them by murmuring, "Will you call worthless one for whom Christ did not disdain to die?"

Don't you see the difference it makes when a man accepts Calvary's estimate upon his soul, however poor and lowly he may be? He cannot despise himself or hold lightly his essential welfare. Nor can he talk cheaply about his fellowmen or be satisfied with low, naturalistic, materialistic or mechanic evaluations upon them. He knows with a profound and deep certainty that members of all races, nations, and classes are more than animals, more than "specks of dust on a ball of mud", more than slaves in an omnipotent state, or cannon fodder in a military system, or cogs in an industrial machine. They are the children of the Most High God, the heirs of His Kingdom and the objects of His love, by nature made for what we are calling Salvation.

Leslie Weatherhead, in *Jesus and Ourselves,* related a story of a friend of his who when a little boy missed his father a great deal whenever the father was called away on important engagements. One night, when his father was expected home, the lad wanted to stay up to greet him, but he had been rather bad, and was sent off to bed. He wakened between ten and eleven o'clock and heard his father's voice, and got up, dressed and came down stairs. Fearing a rebuke for his disobedience during the day, he was still unable to keep away. But when he entered the room his father took him into his arms and held him very close and said, "My own little child." The man to this day remembers the "delicious sense of belonging to his father". Without implying that God is a morally indifferent or Pampering Parent, is there not a fine illustration in that story of Calvary's estimate upon the human soul? *God commends His love toward us, in that while we were yet sinners Christ died for us.*

Thirdly, *The Cross revealed the heinousness of Human Sin.* There at Golgatha sin was exposed in all its ugly, black and foul colours. The legions of Hell were all out on parade that grim afternoon — pride, bigotry, hatred, prejudice, jealousy, greed, indifference, treachery, cowardice, mob-passion, injustice, blasphemy, scorn, irreverence. He who faces squarely the Crucifixion of Jesus Christ will never be able to talk glibly about sin merely being a mistake in judgement, or a maladjustment to environment, or a shortcoming due to upbringing, which more knowledge, more understanding, and more prosperity will automatically remedy. There is something deep and real and terrifying in the very nature of sin, which puts it in determined opposition and resentment towards God, and which aims at nothing short of dethroning

God. In the "impious war" which wages in the universe it is out to kill everything good, true, beautiful, holy and loving. Sin is anti-good, anti-Christ, and anti-God. That is the revelation of sin which we have in the Cross.

Hence, the man who said, "The Cross is presented to our consciences and not to our sympathies and tastes," had grasped its moral significance. We are not asked to drop a sympathetic tear over the scene of Christ's passion. In fact His words to the women along the Via Dolorosa were, "Weep not for me, daughters of Israel, but weep for yourselves, and for your children." If there are any tears to be shed we had better shed them for ourselves. Christ does not need them and we do. Our moral and spiritual degradation, as exposed at Calvary, is something pitiable enough to break our hearts. As we stand before the Cross and see ourselves in contrast to the Pure and Holy One, and in consort with the foul and evil one, if there remains an atom of manhood within us we are driven to cry out as Peter, "Depart from me, O Lord, for I am a sinful man," or as the publican, "God, be merciful to me, a sinner." This has been the experience of countless men and women in history who have been driven away in revulsion and repentance from their life of sin and shame, to find in Christ a new life of holiness and love. The Cross in its revelation of the heinousness of sin effects a work of Salvation.

> *And from my smitten heart, with tears,*
> *Two wonders I confess —*
> *the wonder of His glorious love,*
> *And my own worthlessness.*

God commends His love toward us, in that while we were yet sinners Christ died for us.

Fourthly, *The Cross released in the world the Power of a New Affection.* This was the magnetic power which Jesus predicted would draw men to Him. Thomas Chalmers called it "The Expulsive Power of a New Affection". Leslie

82

Weatherhead referred to it as "The Transforming Friendship". Men are redeemed not by getting new creeds, new codes, or new counsel, but by getting a new love, a new passion, a new Master-sentiment. Vital and radical change in life depends upon change at the very centre of life, the heart, from which come all the issues of life. And without such change Salvation is impossible.

Salvation is not the result of driving the will — Augustine's experience proved that. Neither is it the result of moral rectitude, obedience to the law — Paul discovered that. Nor is it the result of correct beliefs and loyal churchmanship — John Wesley's conversion showed that. Salvation is the result of the heart-warming, indwelling, transforming Presence of Jesus Christ within our lives. We cannot be put right with God until the old occupant of the throne of our lives is crucified and a New Occupant, called Christ, is born; until we can say with St. Paul, "I live, yet not I, but Christ lives in me." Then, and not till then, are we saved from sin and self, and saved to God and eternal life. That is Salvation coming to our house! And that is the work of the Cross!...

Listen to one whose heart was filled to overflowing with this New Affection, Thomas a Kempis: "In the Cross is Salvation, in the Cross is life, in the Cross is protection, in the Cross is infusion of heavenly sweetness, in the Cross is strength of mind, in the Cross joy of Spirit, in the Cross the height of virtue, in the Cross the perfection of sanctity. There is no salvation of the soul, nor hope of everlasting life, but in the Cross."

God commends His love toward us, in that while we were yet sinners Christ died for us.

X

HEIRS OF ETERNITY

Thanks be to God, Who gives us the victory through our Lord Jesus Christ.

1 Corinthians 15:57

On the island of Capri in the Bay of Naples an interesting custom is carried out each year on Easter morning. Hundreds of dark-eyed boys and girls gather with small cages, each containing a bird, and as the service proceeds, at a given signal, the doors of the cages are opened and the birds are given their freedom. This custom signifies the liberty that Christ has brought to the spirits of men in His resurrection from the dead. Can we in our time honestly believe this historic Christian doctrine? Is it acceptable to our intellects as well as to our Hearts?

As I was planning this sermon I received a very curt telegram which read: "Regret to inform you X was killed in mine accident today." With lightning speed death had come to a young father of five children, leaving his wife and little ones dumb and desolate. Is there a message of hope and courage for hearts so grief-stricken? Or can we only utter a feeble word of sympathy? In the face of such stark tragedy, the assurance of immortality alone is relevant and helpful.

The death of our loved ones, or our own approaching end, inevitably raises for us the mysterious question of human survival. Then Thoreau's advice to Parker Pillsbury — "Easy now, one world at a time" — is quite unsatisfactory. Unless we are spiritually shallow or intellectually timid we want to face up to the issue of death and its sequence. "He sins against this life who slights the next."

Shortly after the United States had entered World War I, Lord Balfour of England and Henri Bergson of France, two eminent philosophers, came to New York to arouse American interest in the Allied cause. After a great mass meeting, they were invited by Joseph H. Choate to his home, where all three joined in a lengthy discussion. About what phase of the military crisis? About an altogether different subject — the immortality of the Soul.

It has always been the same. Great men have realized that if life is to be lived with a sense of purpose and worth, and our work to have any final significance, our outlook must be beyond this world. We must have "The hint of eternity" in our souls. To be sure, an other-worldly attitude if extreme may distract us from present responsibilities, but an ultra-worldly attitude robs life and history of any ultimate meaning, and reduces it all to a "trouble of ants" enclosed within space and time. It is imperative that we in this age recapture the accent of the eternal if we are to invest this temporal existence with dignity and sense.

Furthermore, if we are to counteract the modern sentimentality and deception about death, we must also recover another emphasis — that death is more than a certainty, it is a tragedy. So far as we humans are concerned we are helpless to overcome it, or to prevent it. Death is a tragic fact — revolutionary, disruptive and melancholy. And not merely because of our finiteness but more especially because of our sinfulness. The distasteful truth of the matter is that we not only have to die, but we deserve to die. Our mortality is coupled with our guilt. Therefore our fundamental need is deliverance from those two grim powers.

Can Christianity meet that need? Has it any word to combat the voices of negation and despair from our materialists, agnostics and cynics? "If a man die, shall he live again?" What about it?

The materialists of course bluntly answer NO. Man, they say, is one with the physical universe and doomed to the same corruption. They agree with Swinburne,

> *That no life lives forever;*
> *That dead men rise up never;*
> *That even the weariest river*
> *Winds somewhere safe to sea.*

The agnostics withhold judgement, but point out that so far as we have reason to believe death finishes man — more than that we can never know. This view was well stated by Robert G. Ingersoll:

> *Is there beyond the silent night*
> *An endless day?*
> *Is death a door that leads to light?*
> *We cannot say.*

And the cynics scoffingly dub belief in immortality as wishful thinking. It is a solace for fearful people like a nipple-bottle for a baby. The belief is held because it is comforting, and then intellectual support is sought for such an unjustified hypothesis.

To my mind, those voices of denial or doubt are more honest and mature than some who attempt to affirm belief in human survival. For example, Lin Yutang, the Chinese-American, talked glibly about the immortality of influence: "We can pluck a flower and throw its petals to the ground, and yet its subtle fragrance remains in the air." For how long, and what about the flower itself? It is true that Abraham Lincoln's influence lives on in every freedom-loving soul, but we want to know if Abraham Lincoln himself still lives. Or other platitudinous theorists suggest that we live afterwards in our children. Where does that leave St. Francis, Phillips Brooks and Jesus who had no children? Let us not confuse the issue of immortality with the perpetuity of the race, or with a vague influence, or anything else so insubstantial. If we cannot be affirmative we can at least be intelligent, and not beg the question or descend to puerilities. The question is, can we believe in personal immortality?

Across the centuries men have argued that immortality is in our instincts — every race has the belief; that it is in our conscience — every man feels that there must be a future moral reckoning, an "ultimate decency of things"; that it is in our affections — we have not been given the high capacity for love just to be mocked at the last; and that it is in our awareness of an unseen spiritual reality all about us. But in this sermon we shall rest our case on other grounds which, to the Christian, make this great belief essential.

First, *The Nature of the Universe*. George Herbert Palmer, on the death of his wife, Alice Freeman, wrote: "Though no regrets are proper for the manner of her death, who can contemplate the fact of it and not call the world irrational if, out of deference to a few particles of disordered matter, it excludes so fair a spirit?"

Exactly. If this universe has created the most beautiful and admirable qualities of the soul only to throw them all eventually as "rubbish to the void", then rational man is the sport of an irrational universe, moral man is ultimately mocked by an amoral system, and love is the victim of cold indifference. But all the evidence seems to point to rationality in the Universe: that we are living in a cosmos not a chaos; that it is meangingful, value-making and trustworthy; that quality counts above quantity, and the finest values will be conserved. To think otherwise is to fly in the face of the greatest seers, to reduce to nothing all heroism and virtue, and to put ourselves in an intolerable intellectual position which makes no sense of

God's world. The unbeliever has a much less reasonable case than the believer. The latter not only has intuition and faith on his side but reason as well.

A statement made by Dr. Harry Emerson Fosdick may help us here: "To be sure, the mystery of immortality is very great. Anyway that one looks at it, this is a mysterious universe, but I beg of you get the mystery in the right place. It's not so much in the survival of spiritual life that is the mystery; it is the arrival of such a life in the first place, that it is here now in souls whom we have known and loved. There is the mystery — the arrival of a quality of living, essentially timeless and eternal. Would it not be a mystery if, having arrived, it did not survive?" There is the truth in a nutshell.

Secondly, *The Nature of Man*. Man is more than an arrangement of iron, carbon, nitrogen, phosphorus and other chemical properties — he is a person. Man is more than the cleverest of the animals, a creature of greater intelligence and foresight — he is a spiritual being, a living soul.

Thomas Wolfe, in one of his short stories, makes a character say: "Homer...Dante...Milton...Newton...mind of man! Yet when dead — nothing! No good! Seven ten-penny nails worth more!" What if that were the case? If man were but "a speck of dust on a ball of mud", or "biological garbage", or "small potatoes and few in a hill"? Then the doctrine of immortality would be sheer presumption.

But according to Christ man is much more than dust or garbage — he is the crown of God's work, capable of aspiration, courage, self-giving and compassion. True, he is also capable of vulgarity, cruelty, selfishness and hatred, but these are further evidences of his fundamental separation from the animals, of his unique capacity for moral freedom. Man has been made to be a child of God, to have fellowship with Him, and to exercise the rights of a spiritual being. Consequently he is more closely and basically allied with the

Supernatural than with the natural world, and is intended for eternity. The Christian view of man, as Dr. H. H. Farmer of Cambridge University stated it, is this: "He is a person standing all the time in personal relationship to God. It is that relationship which constitutes him — Man...If, as is impossible, he could wrench himself out of that relationship, he would cease to be Man. For when God creates a man, He creates that relationship by the same act — without the relationship there would be no man. Taken literally the phrase 'a godless man' is a contradiction in terms."

And so, it is necessary to take into account the Nature of Man when we begin to think about his destiny. If the New Testament estimate of man is correct, then we know that we were not made to perish, but that God has some better and more challenging purpose for His children than bleak annihilation. This is another ground for our belief in personal immortality.

Thirdly, *The Nature of God.* Dr. W. R. Inge once wrote: "Our belief in immortality stands or falls with our belief in God." That statement has Scriptural support. Undergirding the belief in immortality is the belief in a good, just and merciful God — it all depends upon His character.

Turn to the New Testament. God is there portrayed as our Heavenly Father Who is full of love for all His children, Who numbers the very hairs of their heads, Who watches over their daily lives, Who braves the steeps and darkness to bring them home safely, Who bids His angels to rejoice when even one of His lost sons returns from the far country, and Who treads the Via Dolorosa to the place of a skull on behalf of them all. Because Jesus knew God as such a Father, He took belief in immortality for granted — "If it were not so, I would have told you." Can we not have a like faith? If God is the God and Father of our Lord Jesus Christ, then no evil or calamity can snatch us from His hands, and immortality is more than a

89

dream, it is a certainty.

A Scottish minister and his young son stood one day on a hill-top looking out at the vast expanse in every direction. With a sweeping gesture of his hand the father said, "The love of God is even wider than what we see." And the boy replied, "Well then, daddy, we are right in the middle of it, aren't we?" We are indeed, and because of that we can face death with assurance and hope.

Fourthly, *The Nature of the Christian Life*. William James, the American philosopher, once said, "The best argument I know for an immortal life is the existence of a man who deserves one." That is true Christian teaching. Not that any man, in his own right or virtue, can ever deserve immortality, for as was stated earlier in this sermon, we all deserve to die, and in our sin are helpless to overcome death. But if the life of Jesus Christ dwells in our souls then we are immortal already. The door to heaven is the experience of regeneration. When we are reborn in Christ we pass from death unto life. As St. Paul put it, "Christ in you, the hope of glory;" or again, "If the Spirit of Him that raised up Jesus from the dead dwell in you, He that raised up Christ from the dead shall quicken also your mortal bodies through His Spirit that dwelleth in you."

This is a comforting truth for all who have experienced an inward resurrection, and know that as their life is now hid with Christ in God so will it live with Him forevermore. But it is also a comforting truth for unregenerate souls, who need not fear an ongoing existence bedevilled by sin, egoism and discontent — an altogether unhappy prospect — if such a life has no survival. If, however, God has provided some better way for them, and there is hope of their spiritual transformation after death, that is an even greater comfort. We cannot speak with any confidence about such a possibility, but we can cherish the thought. And we shall, so long as we are uncertain about our own inner state, and so long as we have loved ones whose souls have not been won by Christ.

C. S. Lewis, the Oxford scholar, wrote upon the death of one of his intimate friends: "No event has so corroborated my faith in the next world as Williams did simply by dying. When the idea of death and the idea of Williams thus met in my mind, it was the idea of death that was changed." What a tribute to a life of superb quality! I covet for each of us that kind of life which is its own kind of guarantee of eternal happiness.

Fifthly, *The Fact of Christ's Resurrection.* I call it a "fact" because I know of nothing else which can be so easily verified. Not that there are any ready "proofs" or verbatim reports of the event. But that there is more substantial evidence available. Someone has said that the best proof that the Egyptians possessed great skill as engineers is not to be found by digging up historical documents, but simply by examining the pyramids. Likewise the best proof of the Resurrection is in what it produced. It was by all odds the most creative event in human history. The world has never been the same since. From the Resurrection there followed the birth of the Christian Church, the institution known as the Lord's Day, the conversion of Saul of Tarsus, the doctrine of the Lordship of Christ, and the Gospel of God's redemptive love and victorious power. Like pyramids, these are towering and irrefutable evidences of some great reality or happening.

The disciples never thought of Christ as a memory but as a living Presence, with Whom they had daily fellowship and from Whom they received daily power. In fact, it was this daily contact with Him which was their indisputable proof of His Resurrection. None of them ever claimed to have witnessed the Resurrection itself, but they all claimed to have seen the Risen Lord. The fact of the Resurrection was a logical deduction from their own personal experience of His continued presence. That He appeared to them only in a spiritual form is clear to me, because there is no report of any unbelievers having seen Him — He could be seen only with the eyes of the faithful soul.

Now Christ's Resurrection became for those first Christians a pledge of their own eventual immortality. He was the "first fruits", and as such the promise of more fruits to come. In this victory the "Grim Reaper" had been worsted, and they need no longer fear what his sickle could do to them. Ever after that First Easter Day, they faced life and opposition with an amazing courage, an undaunted faith, and an unconquerable hope. Their victorious lives can be explained only by reference to the Resurrection of their Lord. There is no other accounting for it.

When Michael Faraday, the great scientist, lay dying, a friend came to his bedside and asked, "What are your speculations?" Faraday replied in astonishment, "Speculations? I have none. I know whom I have believed. I rest my soul upon certainties!"

Can you say that? If you can then *All things are yours... And you are Christ's; and Christ is God's.*

Thanks be to God, Who gives us the victory through our Lord Jesus Christ.

XI

SEE YOU IN CHURCH!

As his custom was, he went into the synagogue on the Sabbath day.

St. Luke 4:16

Several times this past week and a half, since coming home to Toronto, I've met people from the church, and our parting shot has usually been: "See you in church!" That is a very common expression, and for most of us — certainly for those of us here this morning — it is a meaningful expression. And I suppose that most who used it in my hearing during the past few days are present here today.

But for many people, the expression "See you in church!" is completely meaningless. They would greet it with a laugh or a sneer, or maybe even with an expletive. I can hear them say: "That will be the day!" A minister said not long ago that if absence makes the heart grow fonder, there are an awful lot of people who love his church. And in *The British Weekly* some time back an Anglican clergyman referred to what he called "the Holy Wheelers": these were the Christians who come to church three times during their lives — first in the baby-carriage, then in the bridal car, and eventually in the hearse.

Statistics reveal that more and more people are absenting themselves from Church and public worship. They have no hesitancy in telling you why. Some will say: "It is a bore, totally irrelevant to my daily life and vocation and interests, and to our problem-ridden modern world. The Church does not deal with the real and vital issues that confront contemporary man — pollution, environmental decay, race, war, hunger, poverty and so on."

It doesn't do much good to try to answer that objection by pointing out that, historically, the Church has made an enormous contribution to human welfare in the areas of health, philanthropy, humanitarian service, liberation, education, et cetera. That's all past history! And it does no good, perhaps, to point out that the supreme contribution of the Church was never intended to be a social-political-economic one, but rather a spiritual-ethical one.

When the Church specializes in the worship of a God of wisdom, goodness and love, how can anyone say that what it is doing is irrelevant? When it specializes in proclaiming a Gospel of the heavenly Father's redeeming grace in Jesus Christ, and of man's own inherent dignity in the sight of God, how can anyone say that it is irrelevant, or that it is doing nothing? And yet many people today suggest that the Church should "get with it" and become more relevant; as though if we were to set up a protest-march every Tuesday evening, and open our halls to all kinds of discussions on pollution and housing, suddenly all the disaffected people would flock back to the church! Don't you believe it!

There are others who say: "I don't go to church any more because it is as dead as a do-do. It isn't where the action is. The action is outside the Church." This reminds me of the story of a little girl whose cat, which she loved very much, was killed by a car. Trying to comfort her, her father said: "But dear, the cat has gone to heaven!" The little girl replied: "Daddy, what does God want with a dead cat?" And so the critics are asking: "What does God want with a dead Church?" Ministers are leaving the Church by the dozens, going into
94

education, politics, counselling, social service and inner-city programmes, because "That's where the action is," they tell us.

But weren't there times in history when the most dynamic and effectual things that were happening were coming not out of the noisy market-place or the inner-city bustle or even the Houses of Parliament or the universities, but rather out of the quiet places of prayer and meditation and contemplation of the high issues and basic questions of man's existence? Is there no place where that still holds true? And is there any kind of action out there, however noisy and frenzied, that is as important as what can happen in here, in the Church?

Somebody else may say: "I don't go to church any longer because the Church kills true religion. Religion is a personal, spiritual matter between a man and his God. As soon as you begin to turn it into an organization and a public ritual, you kill it."

Well, certainly Christianity has its private side. It is a personal relationship and a spiritual thing. It isn't just organization, ceremony, ritual and the assembling of ourselves together. But Christianity also has a public, a social and an organizational side to it. There is nothing so ineffectual as abstract, disembodied, unorganized religion; and not only ineffectual, but usually esoteric or heretical, and severed from the spiritual geniuses and accomplishments of the ages. The Church is as necessary to true religion as an orchestra is to a symphony, as a school is to education, as a government is to patriotism. To talk otherwise is to talk naive nonsense.

There are still others who say: "I don't go to church because the Church, like religion itself, is passe. It belongs to an outmoded time of superstition. After all, we live in an age of science and enlightenment and technological wonders. Man now walks in space and on the surface of the moon. You don't find the scientists in the churches!"

But that is not true! You do find the scientists in the churches — many of them, unless they are psychiatrists or

95

sociologists. Just ask the Reverend Bob Plant down there, who preached to them week by week up in the nuclear area of Ontario. Or think of Sir Bernard Lovell, the greatest British astronomer; Arthur Compton, the American Nobel Prize winner in Physics; or the Oxford mathematician C. A. Coulson. As Dr. Edmund W. Sinott, former Dean of the Graduate School at Yale, said not long ago in *Two Roads to Truth:* "There are two ways to truth. We in science are following one way, but the way of religion is another way, just as valid."

No, I suppose that the average person who no longer goes to church does not absent himself for any of those reasons. He doesn't believe that the Church is totally irrelevant, or that the Church is as dead as a do-do, or that the Church kills true religion. He just doesn't think it is important any more. "It's all right for those who have a taste for it; it's like going to the opera. If you like to do that, then go!" Or: "It's good for the Catholics. They're supposed to go!" And they do go! Or: "It's good for the old people. They haven't much else to do, and they ought to be preparing for their finals, anyway! But it's not for me! I don't see it as one of the important, crucial matters in my busy week. I have many interests, many things to do, and just about the last and least important would be to go to church!"

Well, what do we mean when we say: "See you in church!"? Why should we see one another in church? What's happening here? What's going on? What's the point of what we're doing? Why should I see you in church?

First of all, because *the Church majors in the worship of God.* That is the heart of true religion. Every religion has three essentials: faith or beliefs, morals, or ethics, celebration or worship. And the heart of all religion is not faith or morals but worship. I am disturbed by the way in which the average minister and church member today downgrades the

96

importance of worship. And I am disturbed by much of the talk going on in this city and other places about taxing our churches — not because I'm afraid of the tax, but because I'm afraid of the basic assumption. The assumption is this: that unless the Church is doing something socially useful, as a public utility, it should be taxed. Unless it has a Day Care Centre, groups of A. A.'s, Boy Scouts, a Senior Citizens' Club, and all kinds of things going on which are of a social nature, it is a useless institution and in no way should be exempt from taxation.

That basic assumption is the denial of the heart of religion, of the very thing that essentially the Church does which is unique. There are other organizations which can run Boy Scouts, Day Care Centres, programmes of rehabilitation for alcoholics, homes for retarded children and even schools to teach Christian ethics. But there is no other organization which can major in the worship of Almighty God: this is the unique function of the Church.

One of our modern novelists, Peter DeVries, has a book called *The Mackerel Plaza,* in which there is a modern, new church — a split-level arrangement, with a number of gymnasiums and ballrooms, playrooms and schoolrooms, and anything else you can think of, right up to facilities for crafts and hobbies. Then, at the far end of this complex, there is a small, rather insignificant worship centre. Peter DeVries is making fun of much of our modern concept of Christianity: it is turned wrong-end to!

What is worship? Worship is the heart of religion. During the Civil War in the United States, President Abraham Lincoln attended New York Avenue Presbyterian Church in Washington. I have been there and have seen the pew which he used to occupy. It has been put in the new church — the only old pew in it. One Sunday during service at the point of the announcements, the minister, Dr. Phidias E. Gurley, said: "The Government has decided to close down our church for the duration of the war in order to use it as a hospital." When he finished the announcement, President Lincoln rose in his pew to say: "Excuse me, sir, but this was done without my knowledge, and at this point I rescind that Act because in these dark days the people need to see the stars!"

A church is more important than a hospital, because your living soul is more important than your earthly body. It is here in worship that we hold up and reverence the things which we consider most worthwhile. That is what "worship" means: "worth-ship". It is here in worship that we acknowledge our own spiritual nature and our spiritual needs and hunger. It is in the worship of Almighty God that we confess and face our own frailty, fallibility and dependence. Here we know that we are not masters or gods. Here in worship we raise our flag and declare our allegiance publicly to all the world, testifying that: "As for me and my house, we will serve the Lord!" That has point!

In the second place, I should see you in church because *the Church throws light on life's big questions.* What are they? Well, they are not: "Shall we build a Scarborough Expressway?" "Shall we build a new skyscraper 34 storeys or only 29 storeys high?" Life's biggest questions are not being asked by governments or corporations. They are questions like these: "Who or what is God?" "Who or what am I? — What is my life? Have I any purpose and any value and any ultimate destiny in the scheme of things? Where do I fit in? Do I count?" These are the great questions.

And they won't be answered by Christian ethics and the Golden Rule. We need to remind people who reduce Christianity to morality that they are mistaken. The Golden Rule has no answer to ultimate questions. And the ultimate questions won't be answered by the sociologists. Or by our schools: they may teach knowledge and truth, but they won't teach this subject. The ultimate questions won't be answered by the trade unions: they may talk about brotherhood and solidarity, a fair wage and good working conditions, but they are not interested in ultimate questions. And they won't be answered by governments: they may talk about law and order, peace and harmony, the well-being of the nation and the world, but they won't come to grips with such ultimate questions as "Who is God?" and "Who are you?", and "Where do we go from here?", "What is it all about?"

It is important to note that the New Testament says, *Jesus came preaching.* He did not come as the editor of a great newspaper, or as the President of a great corporation, or as the Prime Minister of a great nation, or as an earthly king. He did not come as a teacher or professor, or as a doctor to heal the sick, or as a social worker to institute reforms. Primarily, he came preaching.

What did he preach? The good news of God and the Kingdom of God — the Gospel which talked about a God of fatherly forgiveness and compassion, a God in whose eyes and concern we human beings matter, a God who has given us a purpose, a meaning and a destiny. And when we come to church and are exposed to the preaching of this Gospel, and not just to comments on the trivia and events of the day, surely we should get a sense of meaning for our lives, direction for our daily work and experience, power to face our trials and reverses, and an inner spiritual liberation and peace, which the world cannot give.

We should come to church because *it is in church that our lives are going to be challenged by the life of Jesus Christ.* You know how easy it is for us Christians to feel complacent out in the world because we're "just as good" as the average person we meet, and perhaps even a little bit better. With all our compromises and vacillations, our egoism and love of expediency, we still stand pretty high in the crowd. It is dangerously easy and comfortable to take our standard of personal evaluation from the world out there. That's why we need to come in here! That's why we need to bring our worst self in and be confronted with our best self. And then have our best self confronted with something better still — namely, Jesus Christ. Then our compromises, and our resentments, our pettiness and greed, our prejudices and hatreds, all stand under judgement! Kiwanis or Rotary don't do that. The schools won't do it either. Or the Lytton Ratepayers Association. Only the Church has this unique function, and it is here that our lives are judged by One so supremely decent and good and loving that we are humbled and then challenged by Him.

Some years ago in a suburban area of an American city, a group of parents got together in the local school to talk about the need for a church. The Chairman of the meeting decided to go round the group and ask each member why he or she wanted a church in their community. One man said: "I want a church here because I want my children to be introduced to life as it is revealed in the New Testament." In his estimate, authentic life was to be found only in Jesus Christ.

I should see you in church because *it is in church that God calls us to dedicated living.* (And summer is no exception! I really don't understand why, if we don't bother to worship God in the summer, we do bother to worship Him in the winter. There is no logic to it!) Our first Scripture lesson this morning was the familiar story of Isaiah's vision in the temple. Picture the young Isaiah: a brilliant, educated young man of the aristocracy, going to the temple because it is a time of crisis in the nation — his able cousin King Uzziah has died. In the temple, Isaiah has a vision of God, high and lifted up in all His majesty and righteousness. In the presence of such holiness, Isaiah can only cry out: "Woe is me, for I am undone, because I am a man of unclean lips and I dwell amidst a people of unclean lips. For mine eyes have seen the King, the Lord of

Hosts!" Then in his humiliation and abasement he suddenly feels the forgiving power of God; a coal from the sacred altar touches his lips, and he is assured that his sins are forgiven. Then he hears the voice of God saying: "Whom shall I send, and who will go for us?" Young Isaiah replies: "Here am I. Send me!"

The Church is the place where men and women have been recruited in every age and generation; where the greatest liberators, reformers and humanitarians have come from. It is under God and in His presence, under His judgement and His love, that they have suddenly heard the call to dedicated living, and have answered: "Here am I. Send me!" It was the same with Jesus Himself. And we read: *As his custom was, he went into the synagogue on the Sabbath day.* The Church is the place of both spiritual survival and spiritual commitment.

XII

REVERENCE FOR LIFE

Over sixty years ago a missionary jungle doctor by the name of Albert Schweitzer discovered what he believed was the fundamental principle upon which civilization depends, if humanity would be properly related to God, neighbour and nature. This principle he called "Reverence for Life".

In his book *Out of my Life and Thought,* he describes the discovery in these words:

Slowly we crept upstream (on one of the long African errands of mercy), laboriously feeling — it was the dry season — for the channels between the sandbanks. Lost in thought I sat on the deck of the barge, struggling to find the elementary and universal conception of the ethical which I had not discovered in any philosophy. Sheet after sheet I covered with disconnected sentences, merely to keep myself concentrated on the problem. Late on the third day, at the very moment, when, at sunset, we were making our way through a herd of hippopotamuses, there flashed upon my mind, unforeseen and unsought, the phrase "Reverence for Life". The iron door had yielded: the path in the thicket had become visible. Now I had found my way to the idea in which world — and life — affirmation and ethics are contained side by side.

A

As most of us know, Albert Schweitzer was one of the

giants of our century. At the age of thirty he was a renowned preacher, theologian, philosopher, organist, and authority on the music of J. S. Bach. And yet, at that age, he enrolled in medical school to prepare himself for a life of missionary service in Africa, and after graduation set off for the primeval forest of French Equatorial Africa where he established a small hospital at Lambarene. Except for brief furloughs for study and organ recitals (by which he raised money for his hospital), he remained there until his death in his eighties. As the years passed, he became a symbol of self-giving service, and was honoured by countless universities and writers, and eventually was awarded the Nobel Peace Prize.

For years Schweitzer tried to come to grips with his own ethical and theological convictions in the face of the pain, suffering and meaninglessness that he saw in the world. He pondered long and deeply on the scribe's question to Jesus, "Which is the greatest Commandment of all?", and on the Greeks' debate about the "summum bonum" ("supreme good"). He asked himself why Jesus' choice, "Thou shalt love the Lord thy God... and thy neighbour as thyself", had never sunk deep into the minds of men, or become a power in the world. He felt that mankind behaved as if Jesus had never lived, and that even Christians were mostly content with making a reverent bow towards Jesus, praising His teaching as the "ideal", and then going about their business and living by lesser and more "practical" principles.

The more he thought about it, the more certain he became that people needed a simpler and more easily understandable and practical expression of Jesus' Great Commandment of love for God and love for others. The solution came to him, as we have already seen, as a great discovery. "Ethics," he said, "is nothing else than reverence for life! Reverence for life affords me my fundamental principle of morality, namely, that good consists in maintaining, assisting, and enhancing life, and that to destroy, to harm, or to hinder life is evil...A man is ethical only when life, as such, is sacred to him, that of plants and animals as that of his fellow men, and when he devotes himself helpfully to all life that is in need of help...The ethic of reverence for life, therefore, comprehends within itself everything that can be described as love, devotion and sympathy, whether in suffering, joy or effort." To Schweitzer, "Reverence for Life" as an ethical principle was rational, absolute and universal. And it was the Great Commandment of Jesus in an underdstandable and practical expression by which men and nations could live.

B

At this point I find it necessary to register my disagreement with Schweitzer. To my mind, he claims too much for his great ethical principle, and I would raise certain simple questions. *First,* is it not undiscriminating? It makes no basic distinction between the different levels of life — e.g. vegetable, animal and human. Are we to love the slug as much as the rose, or the rose as much as the horse, or the horse as much as the child? Would it not be more ethical if in India they loved the cow less and the starving children more?

Secondly, does it not lack depth of feeling? There is no way that we can love the dandelion or rat as much as we can love a human being. To love all life equally is to love no life deeply. This may explain why Schweitzer himself was a somewhat remote person with very few close friends. And along with his ethical principle being undiscriminating, it might explain why he never was much troubled by the social and racial problems of the black people, and apparently saw nothing wrong in his own treatment of them as children, and not as adults.

Thirdly, does his ethical principle not overlook the source of all Christian morality, namely, the act of God in Jesus Christ? The dignity of all life, and especially of human beings, is not the consequence of man's reasoning about nature and humanity, but of what God did when He took our form and flesh upon Himself, and identified with the world of struggle and pain, suffering and death. Schweitzer's principle of "Reverence for Life" cannot account for his own dedication in becoming a medical missionary in Africa, and is quite inadequate to motivate costly sacrifice, personal identification with others, undiscourageable good will and forgiveness. In fact, it is closer to the Commandment *Thou shalt not kill* than to the Great Commandment *Thou shalt love the Lord thy God...and thy neighbour as thyself.*

But with those questions and objections, let us return to a positive assessment and application of "Reverence for Life". And let us not be turned off by Schweitzer's own inadequate, if not benighted, treatment of the Africans under his paternalistic supervision. Most great figures have had their flaws and blind spots. For example, Winston Churchill viewed India as a bright jewel in the British Crown and voted against her independence when Clement Atlee and the Labour Government pressed the issue. Franklin D. Roosevelt never touched the race problem in the United States, and never even brought about complete integration of the races in the Armed Forces. And Martin Luther's attitude toward the Jews would definitely be called anti-semitic by most Christians in our western world today. Like these three giants of humanity, Albert Schweitzer had his faults, and yet we dare not forget the fact that he gave his whole life for over fifty years for God's black children, renouncing the realms of scholarship, music and European culture for the loneliness, hardship, and intellectual impoverishment of the African jungle.

C

Well, then, for our purposes, Albert Schweitzer's ethical principle, "Reverence for Life", is both relevant and basic. He makes these important points: 1) that all life is sacred and belongs to God — all life, vegetable, animal and human; 2) that man is not an isolated creature or form of life, and is unable to sever his ties with nature, animals and his fellowmen, but must recognize his solidarity with all life and live in harmony with it; 3) that indifference and heartlessness towards other life are among our worst sins, like exploitation and slaughter, and should be replaced by empathy, compassion and sympathy; 4) that we human beings should identify with all forms of life, recognize their unfathomable mystery and wonder, and participate with them in the universal fellowship of suffering and longings endemic in all life which wills to live.

For a few minutes, then, let us note what tremendous practical relevance "Reverence for Life" has to some of the major questions which challenge us all in this critical age.

First, *take the question of war and violence,* since this is Remembrance Sunday. Why is there a new and more sensitive conscience on war in our western nations? It is not because of what war, especially in our nuclear and technological age, can do to life, all kinds of life? And the reasons why many, perhaps not all, of the Vietnam War evaders refused to fight was not because they were lawless, unmanly or unpatriotic, but because they would have nothing to do with dropping bombs and napalm on the people and countryside of Viet Nam. War is destruction and death, defoliation and disease, suffering and starvation. War is anti-life. If we ever talk lightly about resorting to violence, or taking up arms, or going to war, Schweitzer's ethical principle will stand in judgement over us. He well deserved the Nobel Peace Prize.

Second, *take the question of the environmental crisis.* If all life is regarded as sacred, then we cannot knowingly allow life to be destroyed whenever this is unnecessary or preventable. We cannot allow municipal and industrial waste to pollute our streams, rivers and oceans and kill our fish. We cannot allow our smoke-stacks and exhausts to spew deadly garbage into the air, and increase the incidence of lung cancer, emphysema and other respiratory diseases. We cannot allow the destruction of millions of trees, and the indiscriminate use of chemical insecticides such as DDT, which destroy wild life and affect the balance of nature. When the Bible says (*Genesis 1:26*) that God gave man *dominion over the fish of the sea, and over the birds of the air, and over the cattle, and over all the earth,* it means that God has made man his steward or trustee, always responsible to God Himself, and not an exploiter or butcher.

Third, *take the question of abortion.* In essence it is not a medical or a legal or socio-economic question at all, but a theological and ethical one. The basic issue is not whether it is done in a safe and acceptable way, after computing its necessity or advisability from social and financial circumstances, but whether it should be done at all. Fetal tissue is not just a growth in the mother's body like tonsil tissue, but an immature human being; and therefore feticide, like infanticide, has throughout Christian history been considered a capital crime. Hence abortion cannot be condoned for such reasons as zero population growth, small families, economic hardship, or because the child is unwanted, any more than infanticide can be condoned for these reasons. It really comes down to the sacredness of life and, to my mind, can only be justified when another life (the mother's) is endangered. Even then it is "The Terrible Choice".

Fourth, *take the question of alcohol and drug abuse.* The reason why many of us are deeply troubled by the rapid increase in this problem is not because we are "killjoys" or "Puritans", but because we know what alcohol and drugs can do to human lives. Some of us have wept with addicts, and stood by them, and helped them get new jobs, and gone to sit with them at all hours of the day or night — and then in a few cases consigned them to their last resting place after they took an overdose of pills or jumped to their death from a tenth-storey window, or piled their car into an abutment on the highway or fell down the cellar stairs headlong in a drunken stupor. It is not just a question of dollars, and jobs, and headaches, and foolish behaviour, but of human lives — theirs and the lives of others.

Fifth, *take the question of hunger and starvation.* A couple of weeks ago on the same late news broadcast, CBC-TV showed pictures of the senseless and bloody slaughter of calves by frustrated Quebec farmers, and then pictures of emaciated, starving children and adults in Bangladesh. They received hundreds of letters and phone calls of protest about the gruesome pictures of calves, but none about the slower and more painful death of the human beings. Have we become callous about the destruction of human life in so many parts of the world by hunger and malnutrition? How hypocritical can we get when politicians and economists and social workers from the affluent nations can sit down to a six or seven-course meal to discuss the plight of the starving people of the world! Canada has contributed to the wholesale dumping of milk in the Maritimes, and the destruction of millions of eggs in Ontario, and the slaughter of calves in Quebec, and in the cutting off of wheat production in the prairies. And yet we have been told time and time again that between 25,000,000 and 75,000,000 persons will die from starvation during the next few years if prompt and effective action is not taken now to alleviate the world food crisis.

Are we as Christian Canadians prepared to question the goals of an economic system which urges us to consume and waste extravagantly, rather than to share available food resources? Are we prepared to modify our affluent eating
108

habits, and especially an excessive consumption of meat? Are we prepared to increase the purchasing power of the poor countries by paying just prices for their exports? Are we prepared to support environmental policies which would provide more food, better trade agreements, more concessional sales of wheat to poor nations at below-market prices, an increase in the purchasing power of low-income Canadians, and a new marketing system for the just distribution of more food — one that serves people first?

Surely it is clear to us that Albert Schweitzer's ethical principle "Reverence for Life" has profound and disturbing relevance for our modern society, not only regarding the five problems that I have mentioned, but also on such other problems as racism, political oppression, economic injustice, urban decay, over-population, cybernetics, microbiology, genetic engineering, psychological manipulation, and the fractured family. We need to be reminded continually that all life is sacred and belongs to God, that man dare not sever his ties with nature, animals and his fellowmen, and that the road to Hell is paved with heartlessness and indifference, and that the road to hope is the way of empathy, compassion, involvement and love. Let us hear the Bible. The Psalmist says: *Let everything that has breath praise the Lord! (Psalm 150:6).* St. Paul says: *None of us lives to himself, and none of us dies to himself (Romans 14:7).*

And let us hear John Donne:

No man is an Island, entire of itself; every man is a piece of the Continent, a part of the Main; if a Clod be washed away by the Sea, Europe is the less, as well as if a Promontory were, as well as if a Manor or thy friends or thine own were. Any man's death diminishes me, because I am involved in Mankind. And therefore never send to know for whom the bell tolls. It tolls for thee.

XIII

ABORTION AND CHRISTIAN ETHICS

Glanville Williams, a British criminologist, made the statement not long ago that abortion should be treated just like a tonsillectomy, for it is only the removal of unwanted or harmful tissue. I wonder why, then, there is so much fuss about the question of abortion if Glanville Williams is correct? Why there is no unanimity among doctors and lawyers and psychologists, social scientists and theologians and ethicists? The International Conference of Abortion, convened under the auspices and sponsorship of Harvard University and the J. P. Kennedy Jr. Foundation a few years ago, included some of the world's leading medical men, lawyers, social scientists, news commentators, theologians, moral philosophers, and so on. When this Conference published its findings in a book, which I have in my study, it called it *The Terrible Choice: The Abortion Dilemma.* Evidently, these men and women from many parts of the world didn't agree with Glanville Williams that abortion should be treated just like a tonsillectomy. Indeed, they made three preliminary and basic points about the difference between abortion and tonsillectomy:

1) Fetal tissue, unlike tonsil tissue, is unique.
2) Fetal tissue, unlike tonsil tissue, is different from the parent organism. A brand new genetic pattern has been created.
3) Fetal tissue is not just a growth in the mother's body

like tonsil tissue but a potential human being from the first week (at the blastocyst), and an immature human being after 12 weeks. At 6 weeks all the organs are there being formed. From 8 weeks on there are no major changes in structure and pattern. At 12 weeks there is activity, the arms and legs move and there may even be sucking of the thumb. At 20 weeks if this fetus were born he would be a "preemy", a premature child, weighing roughly a pound and being about 12 inches in length.

And so, there is no way, according to the International Conference on Abortion, that abortion can be treated like a tonsillectomy.

The United Church, at its General Council meeting in Niagara Falls in January and early February 1971, dealt with the question of abortion and passed certain recommendations for liberalization of the abortion laws in Canada. There was immediate protest from coast to coast by United Church members, letters came pouring in to *The Observer,* and eventually an editorial article by the two editors of *The Observer,* Dr. Forrest and Mrs. Clarke, suggested that the Council set up a task force to do a new study and present a new report. A task force was set up and at Saskatoon last August [1972] there was a second report, followed by much debate. I wasn't there, I was off in Nova Scotia at my cottage, but I followed what came over the radio and in the newspapers, and, eventually, when I got home I received the Record of Proceedings of what had taken place at the General Council. The majority report was followed by a minority report presented by a group of people who could not in good conscience agree with the majority report.

The majority report of the General Council of the United Church made the following points:

1) It affirmed the inherent value of human life in the fetus.

2) It therefore concluded that abortion is always a

moral issue.

3) It further concluded that abortion is to be permitted only in extreme medical, social, and economic situations and always as a lesser of two evils.

4) It asked the Government of Canada to repeal the law which requires a hospital Therapeutic Abortion Committee to authorize abortion.

5) It suggested that up to 12 weeks of age of the fetus abortion should be a personal matter between a woman and her doctor. (There seems to me to be a tragic inconsistency here between this point and the first three preliminary points since the woman and the doctor alone would decide the "extreme conditions" and whether or not the "lesser of two evils" should be entered upon.)

6) After 12 weeks of age of the fetus a second doctor should be consulted and then the three of them, the two doctors and the mother, would have the right even with a 20 week old fetus, which if born prematurely would actually be *a* premature child, to decide to proceed with an abortion. (To my mind, this would give excessive authority to three people on what is "always a moral issue" and "always a lesser of two evils".)

This majority report by the General Council is pretty much the same as the position taken by the Canadian Medical Association, the Ontario Teachers' Federation, the National Council on the Status of Women, the Jewish Women's Council, the national board of the Y.W.C.A., and several other groups.

The minority report submitted to the General Council and registered in the record of proceedings, is to the effect that abortion should only be permitted when the life and health of the mother are in danger.

As Christians, whether we are theologians, ethicists, preachers, or lay members, we are expected surely to look at the question of abortion from a Christian point of view, in other words, Christianly, and not just in our professional roles as lawyers, sociologists, doctors, etc. We are not to take our guidance from Peter Newman of *Maclean's,* who suggests that the question has been discussed enough and let's get on with the business and liberalize the laws concerning abortion; or from Ken Lafoli who, when he was editor of *Maclean's,* said that on the question of abortion, "religion was overruling sanity;" or from the *Globe and Mail* which, in an editorial in January of this year, suggested that Canada should take note of the recent liberalization by the Supreme Court of the United States and that we should at once remove any sense of shame or guilt from the question of abortion. To do that, of course, would be tantamount to saying that it is an amoral (or non-moral) issue, outside the concern of Christian theology and ethics, and only a question of legality, medical science, psychology, sociology, and economics.

As a Christian I must not look at the question of abortion without first giving priority to certain preliminary, fundamental, Christian affirmations. Here they are:

1) God is the creator of man and the only author of life.
2) Man is made in the image of God, a spiritual being.
3) Each individual human being is precious in the sight of God.
4) Man is the steward of life and not its master, and, therefore, holds it in trust as a gift, not to do with as he wishes but always as accountable to God its creator.
5) Human life at each and every stage of its growth and development is sacred and should be protected by society.
6) The Christian law of love applies to the unborn fetus just as it applies to the newborn infant or to any child or adult.

This is why, when Christianity came in ascendancy in the Greco-Roman world, it prohibited abortion and infanticide, and the *Didache,* which was the ethical guide for

113

Christians, declared that feticide or abortion, like infanticide, was a capital crime. In successive generations the greatest theologians in Christian history have agreed. They may not have held that feticide was as great a crime as infanticide, as we may not hold that infanticide is as great a crime as homocide, but they did pronounce it a capital crime. Across the centuries this position has been supported not only by Roman Catholic theologians but by Martin Luther, John Calvin, Karl Barth, Dietrich Bonhoeffer, Paul Ramsay, and many modern theologians. As Christians, we must take into serious account both Christian principles and values and Christian history. They must not be replaced by secular, humanistic, or non-Christian considerations.

Now then let us look at three possible choices open to us. First, there is the non-religious position that abortion is not a moral issue any more than a tonsillectomy operation is a moral issue, and should, therefore, be removed totally from the criminal code. When religion tries to "overrule sanity" let us declare it to be "ultra vires" and tell the ministers to "button up". Then there is the second position, which the General Council took in its majority report, that abortion is always a moral issue and only to be taken as the lesser of two evils, but that in a number of circumstances it may be warranted. The third position, taken by the minority group at the General Council, agrees of course that abortion is a moral issue, and sometimes the lesser of two evils, but only in a case where the health and life of the mother are in danger. This is closer to my own position than the other two alternatives, if I read the report correctly. And, as a preacher, I think it is my responsibility to tell you where I stand on this important moral issue. You too must make up your own minds from a Christian point of view and not from the newspapers, secular magazines, or the majority reports of either secular or religious bodies.

Let us now look as some of the "evils" which are supposed to be greater than the "lesser evil" of abortion. Take,

114

for example, zero population growth — the world has enough people now. There are too many people in China, too many people in India, and in many other parts of the world. Overpopulation is an imminent danger to the human race in the next few decades. Let us legalize and practice abortion as a preventive measure. But surely such an extreme solution can only be recommended by those who do not consider abortion to be a real moral issue. And would they not eventually perhaps include other, even more extreme measures such as infanticide, and euthanasia for the terminally ill, the old, the mentally retarded, and defective new-born children?

Or take the argument which we hear over and over again that every child should be wanted, and that it is immoral to bring into the world an unwanted child. Does this mean that this should become the overriding principle? Could it then not be extended to include all unwanted children, unwanted imbeciles, senile adults, and other human nuisances, burdens, and drags on families and society generally?

Or consider abortion where there is a large possibility of the baby being born seriously defective. The Conference at Harvard University declared that medical science, except in rare instances, cannot predict that a baby will be born with serious defects. About ten years ago there were 4 million thalidomide pills sold to women in Canada and between 50 and 70 babies born were defective physically, not mentally. Should all the others, perhaps 20,000, that were born of women who had taken the thalidomide drug, have been aborted? Is it not possible that one of the children born with some sort of physical defect might be a Helen Keller, who was born blind, deaf and dumb, an Earle Bailey, the distinguished Nova Scotia artist who was born without any feet or legs, or a Charles Steinmetz, dwarfed and misshapen in body with defective eyesight, who became one of the greatest scientists of his day? And is it not possible that all these babies can live a worthwhile and enjoyable life?

Or what about abortion in extreme sociological and economic conditions of poverty and large families? Are we so bankrupt of tactics and strategies that we would resort to such an easy solution as abortion or feticide? Is not feticide certainly after 12 weeks, almost as great a moral offence as exposing newborn infants of large families to death? Let us not shudder at the one and condone the other. Is it not true that there are no unwanted babies being born in Canada, because there are many families waiting to adopt children and cannot get them? Abortion cannot be justified as a birth control measure for the sexually overactive, irresponsible, careless, or ignorant. And this is what is happening today when so many of the abortion cases are repeats (one young woman at age 20 has already had six abortions). One can be excused for referring to our present situation, in the words of a doctor, as "the right to indiscriminate killing" — and all done in the name of "extreme medical, social, and economic situations" as the lesser of two evils.

But what about abortion in the case of rape or incest? If the case were reported and treated early enough it would not be necessary to have an abortion. And unless the health of the woman is jeopardized, abortion is unwarranted — two wrongs do not make a right. Abortion is always a serious moral issue and is not to be resorted to as a legal and medical tactic to "fix" a problem or solve an unfortunate situation. For us Christians it must always involve our most deeply held beliefs about God, human life, our stewardship, and the protection of the helpless.

If we liberalize our approach to abortion to include so many changes and so many grounds for which it can be done, there will inevitably come a hardening of our own attitudes and our own souls. Particularly liable to this would be doctors and nurses who were in constant work in aborting babies. There would follow a gradual lessening of the estimate upon the value, dignity, and sanctity of human life. This would pose a threat to all life, especially to that of the helpless, the infrim, the old, and the retarded. And what about such Christian values as compassion, tenderness, and sacrifice? Would we not be putting a premium on the pleasure principle of the ancient Hedonists — that anything that causes discomfort, burdens, pain, and suffering must be eliminated no matter what the theological or moral cost might be? A gradual reversion to a pre-Christian estimate of life would soon result in a neo-secular and godless culture. Already infanticide is "on our doorstep". Not only are unborn children being destroyed in ever-increasing numbers (the figures are going up rapidly), but children already born with certain defects are being "allowed to die a natural death" as well. Doctors with conscience are burdened enough now trying to preserve life without getting involved in a multiplicity of questions of when to terminate it. And it is utterly inconsistent for secularists and humanists who exhibit such concern for the abolition of capital punishment for murderers, to show little or no interest in innocent fetuses or to object to the introduction of moral and theological values into the abortion debate.

Personally, I do not look forward to a society which refuses to protect the helpless, unborn fetus. I'd be afraid of what it would do to the rest of life. I do not look forward to a society which leaves the matter to private conscience. We don't leave infanticide and homocide to individual choice and private conscience. Therefore, I disagree with the majority report of the General Council of the United Church of Canada. I disagree with the Canadian Medical Association and the National Council on the Status of Women. I repudiate abortion as a policy to keep the population down. I repudiate abortion as a method of birth control. I repudiate abortion as the way to solve some of our socio-economic problems and some of our difficulties with the defective and the unwanted. I repudiate abortion except in a case where the life and continuing health of the mother are in danger, and then it

117

becomes a choice between two lives and we have to choose the life of the mother. Then it's a lesser of two real evils when we abort the baby. And that is *The Terrible Choice: The Abortion Dilemma,* as the International Council on Abortion called it. In a democratic society where each and every citizen bears a measure of personal responsibility for misgovernment, bad laws, or wrong policies, it is incumbent upon us as Christians to exercise our influence for what, under God, we consider to be right. In the words of the New Testament: "Whatever you are doing, whether you speak or act, do everything in the name of the Lord Jesus...put your whole heart into it, as if you were doing it for the Lord and not for men."

XIV

PEACE OF MIND THE CHRISTIAN WAY

Peace I leave with you, my peace I give to you.
St. John 14:27

Then came Jesus, the doors being shut, and stood in the midst, and said "Peace be unto you."
St. John 20:26

"Peace of mind" was the popular theme for preachers and writers a decade or more ago. The very words, as a title for Rabbi Joshua Loth Liebman's book, made it an instant best seller. Norman Vincent Peale promised peace of mind — through positive thinking, pseudo-psychology, and a careful selection of suitable Bible texts on faith and prayer — and packed his church every Sunday, commanded large fees for speaking engagements, and became a wealthy man from the sale of his books. Billy Graham talked about "peace of soul" and assured his vast audiences that this blessing could be theirs with a dose of negative thinking about their sins and a return to God by repentance. Bishop Fulton J. Sheen, perhaps a more scholarly and a smoother speaker and writer than Peale and Graham but less credible, appealed to much the same kind of people as they did, combining the cliches of reassurance and redemption. That was the heyday for that kind of personal religion.

Things began to change in the sixties. Critics pointed to

the deficiencies and distortions, self-centredness and unhealthiness in that interpretation of Christianity. Social activists condemned it as an irresponsible flight from reality, in a day teeming with such problems as war, racism, economic injustice, political oppression, pollution, over-population, hunger and disease. They told us that to seek peace of mind in this kind of world was ethically indecent. The Christians we should be listening to were Rheinhold Niebuhr, Dietrich Bonhoeffer, Alan Paton and Martin Luther King Jr., whose Lord was "The Man For Others". To the activists, Peale, Graham, Sheen and their kind were has-beens, irrelevant tinkling cymbals — at best respectable distractions, and at worse false prophets crying, "Peace, peace," when there was no peace. Except amongst a minority of affluent Western Christians, the emphasis was now on social or "relevant" religion.

Why is it that we Christians cannot seem to grasp the gospel of Jesus Christ in its wholeness, as being both personal and social? As soon as we stress one half to the neglect of the other, we distort the gospel and misrepresent our Lord — and set in motion a force which will inevitably swing to the opposite extreme. We do not produce many like William Temple, who could write *Christianity and Social Order,* and also the devotional masterpiece *Readings in St. John's Gospel;* or like Walter Rauschenbusch, the great theologian of the social gospel, who also wrote a beautiful book of prayers for personal religious use.

A

If my understanding of the Bible is correct, certain preliminary statements can be made with assurance.

1) *Personal peace of mind is a legitimate Christian concern, and is integral to Biblical religion.* In the Old Testament we hear Isaiah saying: *Thou wilt keep him in perfect peace, whose mind is stayed on Thee because he*

120

trusteth in Thee, and the author of the 37th Psalm declaring: *The end of the upright man is peace.* In the New Testament St. John tells us that just before his death Jesus gave his disciples this one legacy: *Peace I leave with you, my peace I give to you,* and at his first appearance to them after his resurrection, he confirmed his promise with the words: *Peace be unto you.* St. Paul and other apostles considered peace to be one of the "fruits of the spirit", included it with "grace" and "mercy" in their triune benediction, and found great joy in "the peace of God which passeth all understanding".

2) *Personal peace of mind for the Christian must never be reduced to detachment, insensitivity, or social indifference.* It should not be confused with satisfaction with things as they are, or the absence of tension, disturbance and struggle. If this happens, it deserves the Marxist label of "an opiate", because it is a clear renunciation of a large part of Jesus' teachings in The Sermon on the Mount, and in such parables as those of The Good Samaritan, The Rich Man and Lazarus, and The Last Judgement. It is a prostitution of the Bible to turn it into an anthology for bedtime reading, personal comfort and reassurance, and to expurgate its "hard sayings" and prophetic blasts and challenges. The only peace a Christian is entitled to is the one with a cross at the heart of it.

3) *Personal peace of mind for the Christian is not dependent upon favourable worldly circumstances.* It is possible in the midst of poverty, ill health, and loss of political freedom and security. It does not require the comforts, amusements, rights, and securities that most of us here enjoy — nor does it necessarily accompany them. If it did, Jesus could never have given it to his disciples, because he would not have had it to give. Let us not forget that it was under the shadow of a Roman cross, awaiting him at the place of the skull, that Jesus uttered the words: *Peace I leave with you, my peace I give to you.* His was not the peace of the cloister or the

sanctuary, but of the crucible and the gallows.

4) *Personal peace of mind in the Christian sense is never to be an end in itself.* The crux of the trouble with the "Peace of Mind" cult of the 1950's was that it tried to "use" God and religion as a means for its own end. The Gospel was not recommended because it was true, but because it could be put to work — for mental health, social adjustment, and domestic harmony. Likewise faith, prayer and worship were treated as tools or techniques in the idolatrous service of the false goddess of peace (Irene), and many churches resembled drugstores handling prescriptions and marketing pills and potions. If there is one sure way to miss finding peace of mind, it is by pursuing it as an end, making it your goal and your God.

Peace of mind the Christian way is always a by-product of something else. Thomas a Kempis put it this way in *The Imitation of Christ:*

> *My son, now will I teach thee the way of peace...Be desirous to do the will of another rather than thine own. Choose always to have less rather than more. Seek always the lowest place, and to be inferior to everyone. Wish always, and pray, that the will of God may be wholly fulfilled in thee. Behold, such a man entereth within the borders of peace and rest.*

The great mystic understood that self-will, self-importance, and self-sufficiency make it impossible for us to possess inner peace, even when we make peace itself the object of our self-concern and striving. That kind of peace can only come to us as a by-product and not as a goal.

Graham Greene makes this clear in his character Major Scobie in *The Heart of the Matter:* "Peace seemed to him the most beautiful word in the language...In the Mass he pressed his fingers against his eyes to keep the tears of longing in...He dreamed of peace by day and night." He tried to find peace in isolation, in escape, in a lonely office in Africa, in separation from his wife, in falsified police reports, in alcohol, in a mistress, but finally committed suicide in his failure and frustration. Major Scobie not only made the mistake of looking for peace in the wrong places, but also the mistake of looking for it at all.

Peace of mind is an elusive maiden who cannot be won by determination and direct attack. She can only be taken by him who pays her little attention, in his preoccupation with other interests.

B

In the first instance, *Christian peace of mind is a by-product of a great faith,* which supplies our lives with personal meaning and spiritual security. This was evident in the lives of the great Hebrew prophets and patriarchs, who believed profoundly that God was their refuge and strength, that He had made human beings in his own image, and that He was always seeking to have a vital relationship with them. They were under no pall of skepticism which doubted the reality of God and of a purpose to human life. Peace of mind is impossible for a man who believes that there is no intelligent God behind the universe and his own life, but that all is the result of blind chance in a cold, materialistic chaos. Dr. Carl Jung, the famous psychologist, once reported that a patient of his said to him: "If only I knew that my life had some meaning and purpose, then there would be no silly story about my nerves!" Well, the secret of St. Paul's inner peace was that he knew that his life had meaning and purpose. Listen to him: *I am persuaded that neither death, nor life, nor angels, nor principalities, nor powers, nor things present nor things to come, nor height, nor depth, nor anything else in all creation will be able to separate us from the love of God in Christ Jesus our Lord.* It was the same with St. Augustine, who made the memorable statement: "O God, Thou hast made us for

Thyself, and our hearts are restless until they find their rest in Thee."

Secondly, *Christian peace of mind is a by-product of a great forgiveness* — release from the burden of our guilt. In *The Robe,* Lloyd C. Douglas pictures the Roman soldier, Marcellus, after his crucifixion of Jesus, trying to forget what he did by getting drunk. At last he slumps down upon his Greek slave, Demetrius, and cries out: "I'm dirty — outside and inside. I'm dirty and ashamed. Understand, Demetrius, I'm dirty and ashamed." Later on, in reflection on the robe Jesus wore, and in recollection of Jesus' words of pardon from the cross — *Father, forgive them, for they know not what they do* — Marcellus found peace.

There is a direct and undeniable relation between inner peace and Divine pardon, for any person who is morally alive and sensitive. Jesus made this clear when he said to the sinful woman: *Your sins are forgiven; go in peace.* And a modern psychologist once said: "I always send my patients to hear Dr. ...... preach: he preaches the forgiveness of sins." A Christian cannot, and should not, have peace of mind, until he has squarely faced his sin and guilt and gratefully accepted God's forgiveness.

Thirdly, *Christian peace of mind is a by-product of a great commitment.* This can best be seen in the account of Jesus praying in the Garden of Gethsemane the night before his arrest and death. In agony of soul, he cried out: *O my Father, if it be possible, let this cup pass from me.* Not until he was able to add: *Nevertheless, not my will but Thine be done* did he regain his composure, and rise from his knees to face his arrest, trials, scourging and crucifixion, with incredible serenity. Self-will, personal ambition, and self-concern are enemies of inner peace.

Matthew Arnold once remarked that the greatest sentence in all literature was Dante's statement: "In Thy will is our peace." Well, Dante did not come to that understanding without a great struggle. Years earlier he had approached a monastery door and knocked three times, until a monk came and asked him what he sought. His answer was: "I seek peace." But Dante did not find peace, not even in the monastery, until he stopped seeking for it, and surrendered himself to the will of God.

We human beings resemble a grandfather's clock. If the pendulum is disconnected, there is a great whirl of wheels and a lot of feverish activity, but nothing worthwhile happens. When the pendulum is attached, everything works in harmony and regularity — the clock is at peace, because it is connected with the elemental force of gravity in the universe. Our lives must be connected with God Himself, The Life of the universe; and His will must become ours, if we are to know peace.

Fourthly, *Christian peace of mind is a by-product of a great hope.* Albert Camus was right on target when he said in *The Plague*: "There can be no peace without hope. Jesus' disciples discovered this truth when their leader was crucified as a criminal, and his cause washed up. They had trusted in his leadership, and had high hopes for his furture, but the whole thing had fizzled out in a pathetic and cruel anti-climax. No wonder they withdrew from public scorn, and hid themselves in an upper room behind locked doors.

Then, strangely, in the midst of their pessimism and agitation, Jesus appeared alive, and uttered four short words: *Peace be unto you.* Suddenly the doors were unlocked, the windows flung open, the lamps set ablaze, and these weak, beaten, frightened men became bold, fearless and strong. They had been given a "lively hope by the resurrection of Christ from the dead". From that day on they declared to men and women everywhere throughout the Empire that the "God of Hope" was the "God of peace".

It was not that they were imbued with worldly hopes of

materialistic and social progress, and favourable circumstances for themselves, but that they now knew that, "come hell or high water", God's cause could not ultimately fail, and love, truth and goodness would not be forever at the mercy of hatred, lies and evil. And they knew that in all kinds of conditions they could rely on inexhaustible reserves of spiritual resources. One of their favourite words was *dunamis*, "power", and St. Paul spoke for most of them when he said: *I know how to be abased, and I know how to abound...I can do all things through Christ who strengthens me.*

I remember reading some years ago about two artists who were asked to paint their conception of peace. One came up with the picture of a quiet lake, nestled deep among tall trees, with the light of the moon on its placid surface. The other painted the rugged, fearsome Niagara Falls on a windy day, with the spray flying in all directions, and a small, snarled tree bent over the raging waters. On an extended limb of the tree was a little bird, singing its song from its precarious perch.

The second artist's conception of peace is the only kind of peace a follower of Jesus can ever know. It is not tranquility, or detachment from this troubled world, but an inner sense of stability and repose, in the very midst of life's tensions and trials. That it the only kind of peace Christ can confer because it is the only kind he himself ever possessed.

Peace does not mean the end of all our striving,
Joy does not mean the drying of our tears;
Peace is the power that comes to souls arriving
Up to the light where God Himself appears.

G. A. A. Studdart Kennedy

ONE

HERESIES COMMON TO THE MODERN LAYMAN

Some years ago Dorothy Sayers, the English mystery-story writer and author of *The Man Born to be King,* said to a group of clergymen: "It is fatal to assume that everybody knows quite well what religion is, and needs only a little encouragement to practise it. The brutal fact is that in this Christian country not one person in a hundred has the faintest notion what the Church teaches about God or man or society or about Jesus Christ."

Peter T. Forsyth said substantially the same thing back in 1909 in the opening chapter on Lay Religion, in his great book *The Person and Place of Jesus Christ.* The situation, however, has grown much worse in these last few decades, and "The spread of religion has cost us the depth of it."

The sad truth is that most people today, even most church-goers, have never really heard the Gospel — just diminished, watered-down, sentimentalized substitutes for the Gospel. As a result the average Christian layman in our time confuses and equates Christianity with religious sensibility, admiration for Jesus, the Golden Rule, love of neighbour, social service, to say nothing of democracy, free enterprise, Western culture, positive thinking, and Rotaryism. Consequently he misinterprets such fundamental Christian virtues as faith, hope and love, and Christian values such as peace, freedom and brotherhood.   To him faith means believing in some vague ideals and religious values; hope means something we should like very much to happen — a wish or will-o'-the-wisp; and love drips with all sorts of sentimental, fleshy, and worldly ideas. Christian peace becomes nothing more than peace of mind, Christian freedom becomes political liberty, and Christian brotherhood becomes formal and legal integration. Of course the great words of Biblical theology — sin, grace, salvation, reconciliation — are only "undecipherable hieroglyphs". As Paul Scherer recently put it, in *The Word God Sent:* "The sermon most readily understood and heartily approved is likely to have in it relatively little of what brought the New Testament into being (the Gospel)." And "The Church most depressingly crowded often hears least of what that New Testament is straining hard to say."

To be frank, the average modern layman cherishes more heresies than you could shake a stick at. He is not only an illiterate in Christian doctrine, he is a deviate, a heretic.

A

There are several clear reasons for his heresy. One is *the prevalence of "Lay Christianity".* Bernard Eugene Meland, of Chicago Divinity School, reminds us that Rudolf Otto and Ernst Troeltsch before himself held that Protestantism "has its roots in the general emergence of 'Lay Christianity' at the close of the Middle Ages, when there was a most potent urge toward what is simple, immediate, and 'understanded of the people' as opposed to theological subtleties and the hair-splitting of experts." But this very venture in lay Christianity, and the demand for a simplified and readily understood faith led to a rash of many kinds of deviations, from the most hidebound fundamentalism to the most untheological humanism. These spawn today in Laymen's Movements and Conferences, and thrive in lodges, service clubs and the Y.M.C.A., with their desire for simplicity, common ground among all faiths, and practicability.

This is not a criticism of laymen as such, nor of laymen's organizations, but simply to warn that in religion as in any other discipline the laymen's version is generally, not always, a popularized and reduced substitute for the real thing — e.g., in Medicine, Science and Music.

Coupled with the emergence of Lay Christianity there was of course *the Protestant principle of the right of private judgement.* This is a very good thing, which we should cherish and protect, but carried to a false extreme it comes to mean that every man's opinion is as good as every other man's opinion. Of course this is nonsense. But it has been the fly in the Protestant ointment, leading not only to crazy sectarianism but also to theological confusion and heresy. To say that a man has a right to his opinion does not imply that his opinion is of any value, or that it is as valid as the next man's. But if we suppose that it is so, and that the opinion of the layman who has done no studying or serious thinking in Christian doctrine is just as good as the opinion of the qualified theologian, we are bound to invite all kinds of weird deviations and heresies — e.g., Russellism, Christian Science, British Israelism, Theosophy, Psychiana, and Mormonism.

In the third place, much modern heresy is due to *faulty communication between the class room or pulpit and the pew.* Most theologians are pretty inept in the art of communication, except to a small group of like-minded experts. And most preachers shy away from the intricacies of doctrine for the plainer paths of moralizing or inspirational pep-talks. Since we all want to be well-thought of, we find it more convenient to let people hear what they want to hear, and to keep their interest with stories, anecdotes, sermonettes, and current topics.

The result is that in order to communicate we revise the Message, and preach something less or else than the Gospel; we accommodate the Gospel to the world, and what comes out is a secularized, homogenized, deodorized revision of the Gospel. If only the theological eggheads could transmit the real things as effectively as the theological blockheads can transmit the false thing our people would be much better informed.

But don't get me wrong. I don't wish to suggest that most heresies within the Church are due to faulty communication of the Biblical faith. It is a serious mistake to assume that if all men knew what the Gospel really is about they would accept it, or believe it. There remains the "Scandal" of the Gospel, and that is not only the offence of the Christian law of love but the uniqueness and particularity of the Christian claims — the Incarnation, the Atonement, and the Resurrection.

B

At this point something should be said in defence of heresy, or at least in explanation of it, when the heresy is deviation from specified doctrines and not deviation from the Gospel itself. "Doctrines are the Church's endeavour to apprehend the truth contained in the Gospel, and as such are human, fallible and wholly subject to responsible deviation." Such doctrines as that of the Trinity or the Atonement are not set forth in the Gospel, but are formulations hammered out by the Church Fathers, in complex and abstruse theological controversy, in order to combat "erroneous and strange doctrine". They were necessary, no doubt, in such days of emergency, to prevent distortion of the faith or the merging of Christianity with certain pagan cults, and to give the faith a sturdy and clear intellectual shape. But, as Professor John Macquarrie, of Union Theological Seminary, New York, recently pointed out, "All theological formulations are approximate...and fall short of the reality they try to express and are, therefore, subject to revision and re-interpretation."

But revision and re-interpretation always carry an

element of risk that must be tolerated — for the sake of freedom for theologians to pursue their work, and for the sake of fruitful debate and a more relevant apprehension of the truth. Sometimes truth will be sacrificed in the interests of relevance, and simplicity, and our reformulations will be revisions instead, but the risk must be taken if the Church is to state its faith intelligibly to each generation or century, and not be content with peddling antiquated terminology. As Macquarrie says, "The only real corrective for bad theology is better theology...and the adult way of coming at the truth is through free and responsible discussion of the issues."

However, the common heresies of the modern Protestant layman are not usually the result of such vigorous wrestling to apprehend the truth, or to re-interpret it in a more meaningful way for our day; nor are there many modern heretics of the stature and sincerity of the great heretics of Christian history. Most of our heresies are the result of ignorance, intellectual laziness, indifference to theological preciseness, reaction at theological pomposity and incomprehensibility, and accommodation with the rationalism, scientism, humanism, and syncretism of our present age.

Perhaps the late Professor Richard Niebuhr's description of much theological liberalism, in his book *The Kingdom of God in America,* is appropriate here: "A God without wrath brought men without sin into a kingdom without, judgement through the ministrations of a Christ without a Cross." Heresies such as these are deviations from the Gospel itself, and not just from hoary old doctrines.

C

The average modern layman subscribes to at least ten such heresies. We can here not do much more than list them.

1) *Too soft a view of God.* "God is love and there is nothing to fear" — that is the central part of his creed. As C. S.

131

Lewis pointed out over twenty years ago, it is not a Father in Heaven that we want, but a grandfather in Heaven — senile benevolence whose plan for the universe is that at the end of each day He could say "A good time was had by all." Lewis went on to make it clear that love is not indulgence, or even kindness as such, but includes moral responsibility which cannot be satisfied simply with the loved one's "happiness": "When we fall in love, do we cease to care whether the one we love is clean or dirty, fair or foul? Do we not rather then first begin to care?...Love may forgive all infirmities and love still in spite of them: but love cannot cease to will their removal. Love is more sensitive than hatred itself to every blemish in the beloved...of all powers God forgives most, but He condones least: He is pleased with little but demands all." And so to ask that God's love should be content with us as we are is to ask that God should cease to be a moral and holy God, and have no concern for our real or essential good — our moral and spiritual well being.

A few years ago Dr. Brown, of the Fundamentalist Baptist Seminary of Toronto, criticized Dr. W. G. Berry and "United Church liberalism" because, he said, we make God's love central and not His justice. Of course Dr. Brown was wrong in his contention that justice is central in God's nature. If God's essence was justice and not love there would never have been any Incarnation and Redemption, any good news except damnation, and we should all be lost. But such a criticism of us as Dr. Brown makes should remind us not to deny or forget God's justice in rejoicing over His love. Since God is holy love, mercy and judgement are two sides of His nature, like the two sides of a coin.

W. H. Auden has a character pray in these words: "O God, put away justice and truth for we cannot understand them and do not want them...become our uncle, look after baby, amuse grandfather, escort Madam to the opera, help Willy with his homework, introduce Muriel to a handsome naval officer."

I was reminded of that caricature by Auden when I read recently what the famous woman preacher of England, Miss Maude Royden, once said about Jesus' use of the term "Father" for God. "It is almost like a pet name," she said. "So endearing, so tender, so familiar...almost more like 'Daddy' than 'Father'."

That's claptrap, if indeed not blasphemy. T. W. Manson suggested that Jesus' use of the term "Abba" for Father was a warm and personal one, but surely it was not sentimental and childish. God is God and man is man; God is the infinite, eternal and holy and man is the finite, transient and sinful; God is the infallible, Sovereign, Creator and man is the fallible, dependent creature; and man only proves that he is an ignorant, silly fool when he does not show proper deference toward His Maker and Ruler. Without the attitude of reverence and humility there is no such thing as true religion. Perhaps we had better be chary about the use of the name "Father" for God, and about references to the "love" of God, until we learn to put moral content into those two terms.

2) *Too naive a view of man.* He believes man is basically decent, kind, and rational. This heresy is as ancient as Pelagius, and has found notable prominence in every period of our western history since the Renaissance and the Enlightenment. Today it is the popular estimate of human nature, and fits in fine with our general mood of confidence in man's scientific and technological prowess. Like Herbert Spencer, we tend "to convert the doctrine of evolution into an instrument of unbridled optimism," about man and history, and resent all such teachings as Paulinism or Calvinism as insults against human nature. The doctrine of Original Sin stinks in modern nostrils.

The only trouble with this optimistic view of man is that it is both contrary to Scripture and denied by history. According to the Bible man from the very start misused his freewill, and brought disharmony into all his relationships. If he could have saved himself, and by himself broken the bondage of his own egoism and repaired the breach between himself and God, and between himself and his fellowmen, there would have been no need for the Incarnation and the Cross. Surely Jesus didn't come, suffer and die to save those who could save themselves!

As we look at human society in this century of global wars, concentration camps, human gas-furnaces, and other ills and horrors, it is sheer blindness for anyone to believe that the root of the trouble is ignorance or illiteracy, environment or the cultural lag, economic injustice or inept politics, dictators or diabolical ideologies. That is too naive and unwarranted a diagnosis. The root of our human predicament is not outside ourselves but inside, not a spot on the map but a spot in the man. As a character in the recent novel *Memed, My Hawk* says: "Every man has sucked raw milk and can do harm as easily as good."

G. K. Chesterton was right: "Original sin is the only part of Christian theology which can really be proved." And it is being proved every day and in every man.

3) *Too light a view of Sin.* A few years ago I worshipped in a Roman Catholic Basilica at the funeral service of a beloved Bishop, and I was struck by the seriousness with which sin was treated all through the service — in repeated confessions of guilt (offences, negligences, frailties, iniquities) and cries for mercy and absolution. The prayers were chiefly for pardon and remission of his sins so that he would not be damned in the wrath to come. Contrast that with many of our Protestant services where sin is hardly ever mentioned — not because it isn't familiar to Protestants, but because we don't take it too seriously. In fact many Protestant services of worship don't even include a prayer of confession — just a brief reference to our "shortcomings" and a short plea for pardon.

Some years ago Walter Lippmann said to Adolf Keller, the Swiss theologian, "Don't forget that the average American no longer knows what sin is." He might have included the average Canadian too. For most of our people sin is either "bad form or psychological," as it is for Celia in T. S. Eliot's "The Cocktail Party"; or it is a mistake, absence of good, social maladjustment, or glandular disorder. But it is not against God or the moral universe, and God, if there is a God, is not concerned with it.

Jonathan Swift once said, "I have never been surprised to find men wicked, but I have often been surprised to find them not ashamed." When we extract the sin out of sin to our hearts' content there is nothing left to be ashamed about — it is a long way from what Carlyle could refer to as "the infinite damnability of sin". But according to the Bible sin is man's most serious malaise, and the root of all his other illnesses and problems; it creates enmity between him and his Creator, and between him and his brothers, and is sets him at cross-purposes with his own better self, and with his natural environment. In the light of the Cross of Christ sin is condemned forever as anti-Christ, anti-God, and anti-Good. Emil Brunner used to say that it was not until we discovered how far down God had reached in Christ to reclaim us that we were able to understand how far from Him we had fallen.

4) *Too low a view of Christ.* An American negro scholar, Professor Vincent Harding of Georgia, recently wrote, "It is we Christians who made the universal Christ into an American mascot." Yes, or we have made Him into Nature's First Gentleman, or a little Lord Fauntleroy, a kindly visionary, or the Patron Saint of Democracy; or into the Wisest teacher, the Bravest hero, the Best man; or lately into "The Man for Others". This is the inevitable result of making much of the religion of Jesus and denying the religion about Jesus. If our Gospel is only the doctrine He preached or taught then He is for us no more than a prophet or teacher; and if it is only the doctrine He practised in his life and sacrificial death, He is for us no more than a splendid example to follow or hero

135

to emulate.

"The essence of Christianity is Jesus Christ, the historic Redeemer and Lord and God, dwelling in His Church's faith." Christianity is a faith in Jesus as well as in His teachings and example. For the Apostles and their churches Jesus was, in the words of Peter T. Forsyth, "the invasive source of forgiveness, new creation, and eternal life", or in the words of the New Testament He was the "image of the invisible God", "the fullness of the Godhead", "the only begotten Son", "Lord", and "Saviour". He was not just a good man, a wise man, or a brave man, or even the best and wisest and bravest man, but the very "mirror of the Infinite", as Canon Streeter called Him.

5) *Too pragmatic a view of Salvation.* It is true that no man is saved by his Churchmanship, his orthodoxy, or his prayers, but wherever did we get the idea that therefore we are saved by our goodness? Surely St. Paul made it crystal clear: *We are saved by grace, through faith; and not by works lest any man should boast.* And Martin Luther made it equally clear, when he opposed the idea of salvation by virtues and good works with the cardinal principle of the Reformation: "Justification by faith alone". Perhaps most Protestant laymen have just as pragmatic a view of salvation as most Roman Catholic laymen do, except that the Protestants have — so they think — a higher list of virtues and good works.

We all need to be brought back to the New Testament truth: that salvation is God's doing, the free gift of His grace, and that it is ours for the taking, no payment required. Lord Melbourne once said, "What I like about the Order of the Garter is that there is no d--- merit about it." So it is with the Order of Salvation, according to the New Testament, you cannot buy it, or earn it, or deserve it.

And yet it seems to be an unknown Gospel, after these long twenty centuries, while what I may call the "Service Club" heresy goes from century to century, and from strength to strength. But God is not a merchant who sells but a Father

136

who gives.

6) *Too utilitarian a view of Faith and Prayer.* Faith is recommended because it works; and prayer too. As the little jingle of a few years ago put it:

> *Faith, Hope and Charity,*
> *That's the way to live successfully.*
> *How do I know?*
> *The Bible tells me so.*

Of course the Bible tells us no such thing, except back in the Old Testament in certain early expressions of Hebrew faith such as *Psalms 1* and *91*. The drama of Job was written to disprove the idea that faith and virtue guaranteed prosperity and happiness, and that misery and misfortune were signs of sin and unbelief. The gospel and Cross of Christ were even stronger witness to the fact that God's sun and rain fall on the just and the unjust alike.

But hardly a day passes without someone saying, in our hearing, "What did I ever do to deserve this?" or "Why do you think such a thing happened to him?" This heresy that we shouldn't love God for His own sake but for what we can get out of Him; or we shouldn't say our prayers or obey the Commandments unless it can be shown to us that they "work" and we shall be rewarded, takes a long time to die.

I am sure that there is too much talk in our day about the power of prayer, because we are more interested in the power than we are in the prayer. William James described some prayers as "lobbying in the courts of the Almighty for special favours"; and Lillian Smith, the American novelist who died recently, described them as "shaking a tin cup in the face of God".

Prayer is not a tool or technique (contrary to what Dr. Peale says) for us to use "successfully" to procure health, abundance, attainment, or a good figure, as the person claimed who wrote a book called *I Prayed Myself Slim*. (William Sloane Coffin suggests a better title for the book: *The Power of Positive Shrinking!*) Besides the blasphemy in all such attempts at "using" or "exploiting" God for our own ends, there are two obvious dangers: that we shall make claims for faith and prayer that they cannot keep or fulfill; and that reactions of disillusionment and bitterness will follow when there are no results or rewards. As H. G. Wells said as a boy in a burst of resentment over unanswered prayers: "All right, God, catch me praying again."

In the words of Kyle Haselden, a former editor of the *Christian Century*: "We ministers are not medicine men with black bags full of specific nostrums, one for each and every ill which befalls man in this world. It is foolish to pretend that we are, dangerous to preach as though heaven were a cosmic pharmacy and we were writers of prescriptions. What we do have is a gospel which declares the will of God for men in this life and which sets before them in all the affairs of this life 'the curse and the blessing'."

Prayer is more than petition: It is adoration, thanksgiving, confession, intercession, dedication, and communion.

7) *Too respectable a view of the Cross.* The "Scandal" felt by the early Christians has been taken from the cross, and it has become a charm, or a "divine object-lesson in self-sacrifice, for people or principles", and not a sacrifice for guilt. We talk about our "cross", and other people's "crosses", just as though Christ's was only one of many. But our "crosses" are not like His at all — they are not sacrifices for guilt. They do not expose the infinite ugliness of sin and call men to repentance, or reveal the infinite mercy of God and proffer men His saving Grace.

The Scottish theologian, H. R. Mackintosh, wrote: "I feel that the great reason why we fail to understand Calvary is not merely that we are not profound enough, it is that we are not good enough. It is because we are such strangers to

138

sacrifice that God's sacrifice leaves us bewildered. It is because we love so little that His love is mysterious. We have never forgiven anybody at such a cost as His. We have never taken the initiative in putting a quarrel right with His kind of unreserved willingness to suffer. It is our unlikeness to God that hangs as an obscuring screen impeding our view, and we see the Atonement so often through the frosted glass of our own lovelessness."

True, but is it a suprise that we do not see things with God's eyes? Or that we are not as good as God? Or that we do not understand the Cross because we are men and not God? Or that for these reasons we shall never fully understand the Cross? Our culpable and basic trouble is that we want a Christ without a Cross — just as Judas did, and Peter, and the rest of the disciples. Like Andre Gide, we feel that the crucifixion obscures the heart of the Gospel — the important thing to Gide was Jesus' teachings and fine life, and not His death. It was different with the primitive Church: The Cross on the Hill rather than the Sermon on the Mount was for it the heart of the Gospel.

On Calvary God did something for us men and our salvation that we could not do for ourselves. He did a work of forgiveness and justification, of reconciliation, and redemption, of judgement and revelation, intended to destroy the power of darkness and sin and to win mankind for Himself. It was much more than setting a good example in sacrifice and heroism, or than exercising a moral influence — to say nothing of an emotional influence — over all who will "stop, look and listen".

On this theme Dietrich Bonhoeffer wrote: "Cheap grace is the deadly enemy of our Church...Cheap grace means grace as a doctrine, a principle, a system. It means forgiveness of sins proclaimed as a general truth, the love of God taught as a Christian 'conception' of God. An intellectual assent to that idea is held to be of itself sufficient to secure the remission of sins...Cheap grace is the preaching of forgiveness without requiring repentance...Cheap grace is grace without...the Cross..."

8) *Too moralistic a view of the Gospel.* To hear even our most literate laymen speak these days one would think that they had never read the New Testament, heard of the works of the great theologians such as Augustine, Luther and Calvin, or even of such modern writers as Reinhold Niebuhr, Paul Tillich and C. S. Lewis. Moralism is our laymen's prevailing religion. Christianity means "doing good", "being kind", etc. — it is a system of ethics, a means of self-improvement or of social betterment, or both. If they would turn to the New Testament they would note that the Gospel is God-centered and not man-centered, that it is Good News about what God has done for man and not Good Advice on what man can do for God, or his fellowman. It has to do with such ultimate questions as "Who is God? What is man? Why are we here? Where are we going?" There can be no Christianity without theology. To divorce ethics and theology, morality and religion, is to emasculate both.

Goodness without God is a pretty barren and thin fare. Not only does it have no answers for man's deepest and ultimate questions, but it has no ultimate justification or support, no eternal validity — it is just an accident in an amoral universe which has nothing to which it corresponds, and therefore carries no ultimate authority.

Even Jean Paul Sartre, the French existentialist philosopher and atheist, agrees that if there is no God there can be no moral values, because we are on a plane where only men exist. He likes to quote Dostoevsky who said, "If there is no God, then everything is allowed."

Moral values are the fruits of theology. Because God is good we should be good. Because God is just we should be just. Because God loves our fellowmen we should love them.

But we cannot do these things on our own — goodwill

needs a profound faith behind it. Goodness without God lacks spiritual resources and dynamic, and is bound to be impotent and insecure. That is why the ethical culturists and practical humanists produce no Father Damiens and St. Francises!

Furthermore, moralism, or goodness without God, fails us both at the point of our moral failures and at the point of our moral successes because it has no word of salvation — no word of grace and forgiveness for our sins and no word of realism and humility against self righteousness in our achievements. We cannot ask forgiveness from the Ten Commandments, and the Golden Rule will not save us from spiritual pride or pharisaism. Moralism has nothing to offer a great sinner like Mary Magdalene or a great saint like Richard Baxter. Though a popular heresy it is an arid and joyless one, hardly the kind to produce evangelists and missionaries, because it contains no good news, and has nothing glorious to herald or proclaim from the housetops and to the four corner of the earth. We cannot imagine St. Paul declaring, "Woe is me if I preach not this gospel," or a St. Peter crying, "There is salvation in no other. For there is no other name under heaven given among men, whereby we must be saved, than the name of Moses the lawgiver or Marcus Aurelius the moral philosopher."

I could go on. There are other heresies common to the modern Christian layman — e.g., too worldly a view of the Kingdom of God, and too cheap a view of the Church — but the eight I have dealt with are as common, and as dangerous, as any. Paul Scherer has said that "We sing more heresy than all the councils (of the church) ever condemned." He shares John Calvin's uneasiness about hymns, that they may contain heresies. It might be interesting and instructive for us to check our Hymn Book in this regard; not that we should go through it with a theological fine-tooth comb to uncover heresies like lice, but that we might eliminate from our Sunday repertoire of hymns those whose heresies are really heresies against the Gospel and not just against certain specified doctrines.

The editor of the *Observer* suggested not long ago that a heresy trial might be good for the United Church. It would certainly compel us to take a longer and more serious look at our theology, and it would emphasize the fact that beliefs do matter. But I am sure the editor was being facetious. Few things could be worse for our Church, or any Church, than a heresy trial. Think of the theological objections to such a trial, and the practical dangers of bitterness, division, inhibition of speech, and the priority given to the letter rather than the spirit of the law. I suppose most members of our Church, and most preachers in our pulpits, and most theologians in our colleges, entertain some heretical opinions, if not against the Gospel certainly against the creeds — because in the last analysis there are no simple answers to complex questions, and no final or definitive solutions to the mysteries of God. But God does not want us to accept, or pretend to accept, what we cannot believe. As John Baillie put it, "Dishonest belief is in His eyes a far more heinous thing than honest unbelief." And theology today is not in a position to throw its weight about, or to claim the possession of the whole truth.

Several things can be said in conclusion: We are all heretics at some point or other; we shall always have heresies in the Christian church, because it is composed of fallible human beings; there are worse things than heresy — apostasy, indifference, lovelessness, and the pride of knowledge and spirit which claims that its brand of orthodoxy is the truth, the whole truth, and nothing but the truth, so help me God.

TWO

HOW RELIGION OBSTRUCTS AND SUBVERTS TRUTH

Some of the worst crimes against humanity have been comitted by religion: the crusades, religious wars, anti-Semitism, racial discrimination, the persecution of heretics and witches, denominational bigotry and cultural destruction.

Who was it that burned John Huss, desecrated the body of John Wycliffe, threatened the life of Martin Luther, and rotten-egged John Wesley? Religionists. Who was it that stoned the prophets, persecuted the Apostles, and crucified Jesus? Religionists. The real battle is rarely between religion and atheism, but between good religion and bad religion. Amos was not opposed by agnostics, Stephen was not put to death by infidels, Latimer and Ridley were not burned at the stake by Bible-haters, and Jesus was not assassinated by skeptics or secularists. History records not only the noble thoughts and deeds of good religion but the ignoble thoughts and deeds of bad religion.

Part of this sad story has been the tragic role religion has played as an enemy of truth — mind you, not an avowed enemy, but an avowed friend: nevertheless, more dangerous and destructive than its avowed enemies. Religion has rarely set itself the task of deliberately opposing truth, but it has all too often effectively obstructed the truth, suppressed it, and subverted it. Claiming to be based on the truth, to be the truth, to possess a given body or corpus of revealed truth, and even to have a special, supernatural line to the fountainhead of truth, it has sometimes betrayed and even crucified the truth.

How? By its official index and censorship on literature, or its restricted education, or its anti-intellectual bias on faith as over against reason? No, not usually, but by loving other values more than the truth. Samuel Taylor Coleridge once said, "He who begins by loving Christianity better than truth, will proceed by loving his own sect or church better than Christianity, and end in loving himself better than all." And Meister Eckhart, the great mystic, put it in these words: "If God were able to backslide from truth I would fain cling to truth and let God go."

Because we have loved other values more than truth, religion has sinned against truth in a number of ways, with serious consequences.

1) *By obscurantism.* Religion tends to make sacrosanct everything it touches, and thus to become ultra-conservative, and overly protective. As a result it becomes fearful of inquiry, criticism, and new truth, which might threaten its values, sacred structures, or institutions. (Father Charles Davis, eminent British Roman Catholic theologian, who recently left the church — with attendant world-wide publicity — charged, among other things, that the church sacrifices truth and personal rights for the sake of its own institutional interest, and for the preservation of ecclesiastical authority.) And religion has often been suspicious of scientific findings, historical and Biblical criticism. How else account for the hysteria in some religious quarters over the theories of Copernicus, Galileo, Darwin and Freud?

Religionists have often forgotten three important facts: a) that all truth is of God; b) that there are at least two roads to truth (if not more) — the road of science and the road of religion; c) that at best we can never know more than a tiny fragment of the truth, as St. Paul said, *We see through a glass darkly* and we only *know in part.*

Every honest and humble man is an agnostic, albeit a believing agnostic. We cannot ever expect to capture truth, or to comprehend mystery. A sense of the mystery of things is the beginning of learning and wisdom. Centuries ago, Socrates said, "Philosophy begins in wonder." In our time Albert Einstein made a similar statment, "It (wonder) is the fundamental emotion which stands at the cradle of true art and true science." Not only is wonder the beginning of learning and wisdom, art and science, but of religion too. In the seventeenth century, Jeremy Taylor wrote that, "A religion without mystery must be a religion without God." Therefore, religion should be open and congenial to inquiry and new truth, from whatever source it may come, and while clinging fast to that which is good and true in the past be willing to test all things, and like a wise merchant bring forth things both new and old. There should be no place in Christianity for obscurantism or the closed mind, or the presumption to final and complete knowledge.

2) *By cowardice.* You might prefer to call it caution, or discretion, but I am afraid it has sometimes been closer to supine pussy-footing. For every time we have kept quiet out of deference for the old folks' feelings, there have been ten times when it has been from fear of criticism or unpopularity, or from fear of disturbance within the organized Church. When Robertson Smith was on trial for heresy by the General Assembly of the Church of Scotland, an Elder of the church, devout and loyal, was overheard to say: "Granted that Robertson Smith is right, if it is truth, it is dangerous truth, and he has no right as a professor of the Church to upset the Church by declaring it."

That is bound to be our attitude if we love peace and quiet within the Church more than we love the truth. The result will be that there will exist a gulf between the knowledge of the pulpit and that of the pew, and that we preachers shall be living a theological double life. When we are together in our

145

seminaries or ministerial associations, we shall talk freely about recent trends in theology and Biblical criticism, but when we mount the pulpit we shall take good care not to "let the cat out of the bag". This will mean that we shall preach topical or textual sermons, but rarely doctrinal or expository sermons, in order to keep from skating on thin ice, lest we inadvertently fall through.

For instance, if we had been honest with our people, Bishop John A. T. Robinson's little book *Honest to God* would never have created the stir it did. Most of us had read of the writings of Tillich, Bultmann, and Bonhoeffer years ago, and we had undergone fairly serious training in the more liberal schools of Biblical and theological studies during our college days, but we had not transmitted our new knowledge — not even a little of it — to our people. We carefully avoided ideas that might be disturbing, and for our own safety or ease, we dared not conduct an adult Bible class where thinking people would put us on the mat. We were not deliberately dishonest, but we nevertheless obstructed and subverted the truth; and perhaps lost more members in the process than we gained or held by our pussy-footing. It serves us right, but it is most unfortunate for God and His Church.

There are still people in our churches who think that when we refer to the Bible as the Word of God, we mean that it contains the word of God; or that when we say that the Bible is inspired we mean that it was dictated by God (to men who were mere stenographers and did not possess any intellectual or spiritual genius of their own); or, that if we maintain that the Bible is infallible, we mean that it is inerrant in every detail, in its science and its history, as well as in its spiritual purpose. We ministers are to blame that such people are the victims of a false, or even idolatrous, Biblicism. They deserve to be told the truth. If the Church is not to become an anachronism in an educated world, and a collection of the ignorant and the gullible, we had better begin at once being honest with our people.

3) *By Dogmatism.* The notion that faith means giving our minds to certain definitive doctrinal propositions, instead of giving our lives to our Lord and Master, has wrought heavy damage in the Church, and blotted history with the blood and burning of the inquisitions and heresy trials. A missionary to Trinidad tells about seeing three little churches all on the same street of a small city: one was called "The Church of God", another "The True Church of God", and the third, "The Only True Church of God". For me, I prefer untrammelled honest-to-goodness atheism to the kind of religion which pretends to kr ow all the answers, and spells them out in pat little creeds, and commits to hell all people who cannot accept them. One of Britain's greatest theologians, Peter T. Forsyth, in *The Person and Place of Jesus Christ,* gave this good piece of advice: "Beware of clearness, consistency, and simplicity, especially about Christ." We dare not be definitive and dogmatic with eternal truth.

Listen to the words of John Baillie, in *Invitation to Pilgrimage:* "Some men say, 'Religion consists in the docile and unintelligent acceptance of a mass of antiquated dogmas'...God does not want any man to accept, or pretend to accept, what he cannot believe. God's demand on me is not that I should force myself to accept a creed, nor is it by my acceptance or non-acceptance of any creed that I shall be judged by Him...What God directly demands of us is...not belief, but 'truth in the inward parts'...Let us not deceive ourselves by saying that Christ wants us to give up the quest of truth and accept Him instead. It is as the truth that He wants to be accepted, or not at all." (page 21) "Dishonest belief is in His eyes a far more heinous thing than honest unbelief. To the perplexed seeker whose most diligent seeking for truth has seemed to lead him away from God and Christ it must therefore be said, 'Do not stop seeking, but look still deeper. Do not stop thinking, but think harder. Do not be less honest

147

with yourself, but more honest.' " (page 23)

Doctrinaire religion has been an enemy of truth, as well as of freedom, love, and brotherhood, because it mistakenly assumes that it is possible to comprehend and define ultimate truth, and then arrogantly presumes that it has done so. As Alec Vidler said, "Theology makes itself ridiculous when it says, as an English Roman Catholic bishop said a year or two ago, 'We have the assurance of our position. We have the certainty of the possession of truth. We have the answers to all the questions'." We need to heed the warning of Alfred North Whitehead: "We must not expect simple answers to far-reaching questions."

4) *By Moralism.* It is well when the three ancient cardinal virtues go together - Truth, Goodness and Beauty - but it is tragic when they separate and try to go it alone. For example, beauty without goodness is corrupting, truth without goodness is cold and uninviting, and goodness without truth is incomplete and impotent.

We have suffered in the church from the divorce of goodness from truth, from the idea that beliefs do not matter, that religion is really only morality, and it's a man's conduct alone that counts. The consequences of such an untheological Christianity are that we neglect or despise the great truths — about God, and Christ, and Creation; about life's meaning, dignity and destiny; about ourselves, and our fellowmen, and our immortality. Truth is sacrificed, and the be-all and end-all of "practical" religion becomes morality - perhaps touched with emotion, as Matthew Arnold would like it, but still only morality.

The result of all this is the decay of true religion. When men love goodness more than truth, it is not only truth that suffers but goodness also. Morality requires theological justification and support, an ultimate ground and an ultimate hope. An untheological Christianity is eventually an unethical Christianity.

148

But even if morality could survive without theology, Christian conduct without Christian truth, that would in no way make the truth unnecessary or superfluous. The Christian faith is not just a "recipe for procuring goodness." It is important because it is true! I agree with Harry Blamires, an English layman, who recently wrote: "For the Christian, faith will remain true whether we who profess it turn into heroic saints or into even more miserable sinners . . .What a mean blasphemy it would be to go through magnificent acts of public worship always with the dominant intention at the back of the mind, 'This is really going to make a better chap of me'!" (*Christian Mind,* page 110) Christianity is to be proclaimed because it is true. That's reason enough.

5) *By Pragmatism.* We have been too concerned with making Christianity work. This can be seen in such prominent modern manifestations as "life-situation" preaching and the cults of peace of mind and inspiration. Take the first, "life-situation" preaching. It has a great deal to commend it, in that it respects the needs of the hearers, and seeks to be Christianly relevant to them. The danger is that we neglect the wider areas of Christian truth, in our preoccupation over trying to fit and fix the message to the needs, supposed or real — if indeed not the wants — of our hearers. We are apt to forget that sermons that never rise more than six feet above the ground are not the most practical after all. Men and women have profound intellectual and spiritual needs as well as moral, social and psychological needs, and the most "unpractical" and otherworldly truths are the most practical for the long haul. In the final analysis, we are not ordained to "help" people but to proclaim the truth of God as in Jesus Christ.

Then there is the "Peace of Mind" cult, which has had such a universal vogue since 1946 or thereabouts. Its main objective is to ease the load of human anxiety, not to proclaim the Gospel. A few years ago when Listen Pope, Dean of Yale Divinity School, criticized Norman Vincent Peale's sermons and books, all the letters in defence of Peale were from people who said that he had done them good. Not one of them thought to say that he had preached or written the truth. That was apparently irrelevant. Dr. Pope rightly replied that it didn't matter whether Peale's pills had done them good or not, as Christian teaching they were not true. Maybe aspirins, or a rabbit's foot, or a psychiatrist's couch, or Bahai will do us good, but that does not make them Christian. Christianity should be preached because it it true, eternally true, and not because it is a useful utility for human beings "cumbered with a load of care."

And there are the cults of Inspiration. Their sole purpose is to inspire, to give people a "lift," to bring them consolation, or reassurance, or good cheer. Surely none of us underestimates the importance of these values, but neither should we suppose that this is the main function of Christianity. Most of the preaching of our Lord was of a sterner stuff. Not only did people like the rich young ruler leave Him, but there soon came a day when most of His followers dropped out because they couldn't take his "hard sayings." There was not much comfort in such admonitions as "repent," "deny yourself," "take up your cross," "love your enemies." If people were looking for inspiration, they could do better by sticking safely to some of the harmless Psalms. And mind you, if we are looking for inspiration in the Bible, we'll skillfully pass by many of its pages. The Bible was never written for private devotions, or as bedtime literature — certain parts will keep us awake all night!

Joseph Haroutunian once said that man's intellectual dignity "has its own inalienable right to truth, even at the expense of happiness or existence itself." Of course, man is a thinking being, a free and responsible soul, and is entitled to more than the morsels of truth that he can easily digest, or that, in our estimation, will do him good or buck him up. God's message in Jesus Christ is true, whether it "works" or not;

whether it cheers or challenges us; whether it comforts or scares us; whether it lifts us up or casts us down or turns us inside out!

6) *By Propaganda.* The Church has learned too may lessons from Madison Avenue, and the Ads and Sales Clubs. As a result, it frequently loses all sense of proportion in its claims for the Gospel, and offers Christianity to people as a wonder drug, which, alas, many of them discovered to be a "gold brick." When we turn the Church into a retail outlet to "sell" Christ and Christianity, or even go into Madison Square Garden and open up a wholesale outlet, to "sell" Him on a big scale, we are treating Christianity as a commodity, or a technique, or a solution. We have seen the gigantic signboards with their advertisements: "Christ is the Answer." We have over-sold that one, until Christ is supposed to be the answer to every ill from mental disturbance to war and social disharmony. If only He were allowed to take over there would be, presumably, no more problems.

But it isn't true. There is no evidence to support the grandiose claim that Christ is the guarantor of mental health, for example, or that a Christian will be mentally healthier than a Buddhist or a pagan. In fact, statistics show a lower incidence of mental illness among Jews than among Christians, and among Roman Catholics than among Protestants. Nor can it it be proved that a Christian lives longer, or has better physical health, than anyone else.

Perhaps there is a lot of wisdom in Dietrich Bonhoeffer's insistence that man should grow up and become spiritually mature, and no longer require a God who is a "deus ex machina", who must guarantee everything, and solve everything, and always come to our rescue or be at our beck and call. It is in this sense that he says, "God is teaching us that we must live as men who can get along very well without Him." We ought to love God for His own sake, and not for what He can do for us.

When I read the New Testament, especially the Gospels, I am impressed with the fact that Christ is often the Question, and not the Answer. He is the Question that God puts to each and every one of us, and to our modern nuclear age. The answer depends on us, and on our world.

7) *By Syncretism.* In speaking to the annual Meeting of the Board of Evangelism and Social Service in 1962, Kyle Haselden, Editor of the *Christian Century,* called syncretism Christianity's subtlest foe. He defined it in these words: "The coalescence of different forms of faith and the disappearances of the essence of Christianity in such a coalescence." Hinduism is a good example of syncretism. It is a kind of religious grab-bag, or sucking sponge, which takes minority religions into itself, and reduces their particular truth to a tiny part of Hinduism's — truth-in-general. For example, when several of the delegates to the Third Assembly of the World Council of Churches in New Delhi visited a Hindu Temple, the Hindu priest greeted them, saying, "Welcome in the Name of our Lord and Saviour Jesus Christ." No problem you see — Jesus and Krishna, the cross and the botree, resurrection and reincarnation — all equal parts of truth -in-general! The result is that Christ is no longer "The Way, the Truth, and the Life", but just another prophet or teacher, and Christianity has no particular or unique truth to proclaim.

In North America, we have our own brand of Hinduism, which scholars like Will Herberg, Martin Marty, and J. Robert Nelson refer to as "Religion-in-General". It is "the idolatrous notion that all religions, anything religious, and all things done in the name of religion are good" Reinhold Niebuhr has said this about it: "Our religiosity seems to have as little to do with the Christian faith as the religiosity of the Athenians. The 'unknown god' (referring to St.Paul's observation in Athens) in America seems to be faith itself." Anything goes. There must be no claims of particularity or uniqueness. God is Mr. "Someone" — who, it doesn't matter, just Someone; and faith is faith — in what it doesn't matter, just have faith. Its theme song is "I believe"; its saint is a Hollywood actress who declared, "Oh, yes, I believe in everything — a little bit;" its funeral hymn is "Beautiful Isle of Somewhere;" its prophet is a "Stranger from Galilee" who was just about the sweetest and most lovable young man ever born, the "spittin' image" of Warner Sallmann's nice painting. And its creed begins with these timid affirmations (Creed of an American Community Church — Marty, page 35): "I believe in God, the Father all-loving; Maker of all that is; and in Jesus Christ, lovelist of his many sons, our friend; who was born of the Mother, Mary; moved by the Spirit of God; suffered under the systems of men; was crucified and died for the sake of truth and right. Yet he lives again in the lives made beautiful by his truth, ascending into the hearts of men, working at the right hand of God, the Father who works all that is good." Such a creed doesn't have much in common with the Apostles' Creed, or with what we commonly refer to as the Christian faith.

Another form of syncretism even worse than the above is the identification of Christianity with our Canadian or American way of life, and our national purpose. I have in my files a Sunday calendar from a Florida Community Church which illustrates this identification. On one page is recorded the attendance of the previous Sunday. Fantastic — it was filled twice. With whom? With everybody — Presbyterians and Christian Scientists, Methodists and Roman Catholics, Baptists and Bahai, Anglicans and Jews — all united in a common faith, in America (not God). On the back page there is an outline of a sermon by the minister. It is called "The Untroubled Heart", and its text is Jesus' great words, "Let not your heart be troubled." Troubled about what? Three things — about Democracy (good old god Demos will take care of it, I suppose), about civilization, and about death. Democracy is the perfect system, our civilization is not bound for the scrap heap but is on the way upward and onward, and death shouldn't scare us because it is "an old door in a garden wall, and on the other side of the wall flowers, not flames".

Such a secularized and untheological religiosity is an enemy of the truth we have in Jesus Christ, because it loves patriotism, respectability, tolerance and unity more than truth.

These then, to my mind, are some of the ways, seven in fact, by which religion obstructs and subverts the truth: obscurantism, cowardice, dogmatism, moralism, pragmatism, propaganda, and syncretism. But they are only the more prevalent, and the more destructive, I am sure. William Penn wrote; "Truth suffers more by the heat of its defenders than from the arguments of its opposers." Yes, not only by the heat of its defenders, but by their other sins and stupidities. Perhaps we could add several stanzas to this ancient prayer:

> *From the cowardice that shrinks from new truth,*
> *From the laziness that is content with half truths,*
> *From the arrogance that thinks it knows all truth,*
> *O God of truth, deliver us.*

"Where are you going, holy man?" a peasant in India said to an old traveller as they stood together under the shade of a tree. The old man answered: "To a city far away." "In India?" the peasant said. The answer was, "Further." "In Asia?" "Further, my friend, further; for that city I seek is Truth and it is hidden in the heart of God."

For us Christians, we believe that the truth in God's heart was disclosed in Jesus Christ, and the closer we come to Him the nearer we draw to truth, and that this is the truth which makes men free.

If this was a sermon and not a lecture I would give it two brief texts for my conclusion: *Behold Thou desirest truth in the inward parts, (Psalm 51:6)* and *Speaking the truth in love...grow up into Him in all things, which is the head, even Christ. (Ephesians 4:15)*

154

THREE

THE CHRISTIAN INTERPRETATION
OF HISTORY

Can we moderns believe in progress? Can we hold any hope for a better world? Dare we be optimistic towards the future? Is human history going anywhere? These are fundamental questions in our age. And they indicate the sort of age in which we live — so radically different from the early years of this century, or from the previous two centuries, or indeed from any other age since the Renaissance.

Ours is a time of pessimism and despair. Its effects can be seen in a frantic search for security, a revival of fundamentalist and individualistic religion, the popularity of pre-millennial "gold bricks" and magic cults such as astrology, and a general worldliness of the "eat, drink, and be merry for tomorrow we die" kind of evasion. These are all resorts for people who have lost hope of human history.

But why this dark mood of despair and disillusionment? Because the illusions which we had cherished for such a long time eventually burst in our faces. We had built our pretty castles in the air, our Utopias and Brave New Worlds. And when we were almost ready to move in and occupy them, something disastrous happened. A monkey-wrench jammed the wheels of progress, "demonic" forces turned things into reverse gear, and homo sapiens' bus broke down with his perfect society just around the corner. All of us except the utopian Marxists, scientific humanists, and unrepentant theological liberals have been led to re-examine our dreams, and to become chastened realists or gloomy pessimists.

Does Christianity have a word of encouragement for an age such as ours? What does it have to say about the historical process and the possibility of progress?

A

First, *we had better ask where this idea of progress came from.* Did men construct it from empirical evidence, or did they deduce it from a philosophy of life or faith? Reinhold Niebuhr said that there was no sufficient objective evidence in history to justify a belief in progress. History, he told us, shows progress equally towards chaos and towards cosmos, and its coherences and incoherences are so entangled with one another that we are unable to discern any clear and exact pattern of events. If we hold a belief in progress, we do so by faith and not by sight; that is, it is a philosophy of life and its roots are in certain a priori assumptions; it is not an impartial conclusion drawn from empirical evidence.

Historians inform us that the savage, primitive cultures had no belief in progress. How could they when they had no written records, no social memory, no cumulative evidence of the past to compare with their present? Later cultures did acquire these instruments of judgement, and came to think that there had been advancement. But let us note that this did not convince them that progress was certain or constitutionally inherent in history. Some of them thought of history as being in the grip of Fate or Nemesis or Kismet, and its final end would be catastrophe. Others of them held a kind of biological interpretation of history, which pictured civilization, like organisms, coming to birth, reaching childhood and youth, manhood and middle age, and eventually old age, decline and death.

But the most prevalent among the ancients was the cyclical theory of history — that history went round as a cycle

156

and came out where it began. Then a new cycle would commence. This was the view of thinkers like Lucretius and Seneca, Pythagoras and Plato. And it was the view commonly held by the Chinese, Indians, Egyptians, and Babylonians. The cycle was referred to as the Great Year, and its length was figured to measure 36,000 solar years. This cyclical view is a pessimistic judgement upon history — always the cycle must run its course to disintegration and decay. Listen to Seneca: "There will one day come an end to all human life and interest...A single day will see the burial of all mankind...When the destruction of the human race is consummated...The ancient order of things will be recalled. Every living creature will be created afresh. The earth will receive a new man ignorant of sin, born under happier stars. But they too will retain their innocence only while they are new. Vice quickly creeps in..."[1] (We may note here that the cyclical view of history was brilliantly propounded by Brooks Adams in his important book *The Law of Civilization and Decay,* which was published in 1896.)

Where then did the idea of progress come from? John Baillie tells us, in his book *The Belief in Progress,* that it arose in two cultures or religions, perhaps independently of each other — Zoroastrianism and Judaism. The former thought of world history as the scene of a conflict between good and evil, which would someday result in the final victory of good and the complete defeat of evil. It is, however, to Judaism that we Westerners must look for the roots of our belief in progress. And there we see that their view of history stemmed from their view of God. To the Hebrews God was no First Cause or Prime Mover. He was the Lord of history as well as of the created order, and history was the continued act of God. Though history was the field of human activity, to the Hebrews, it was also the field of Divine activity, and God was the Chief Actor in every event.

[1] *Physical Researches,* Volume III, pages 28, 29, 30. Quoted by John Baillie in *The Belief in Progress,* page 19.

Moreover, this God who was active within history gave it an ideal goal toward which it moved. No matter how grave the situation or how glaring the evils, the prophets of Israel were convinced of the guidance of God, of His ultimate control over men and nations, and of a Divine purpose in history. They talked about "the day of the Lord" and the "Messianic Age", when evil should be overthrown and a universal reign of righteousness and peace would be established.

This Hebrew conception of history was inherited by Christianity. It is plain that Jesus and His early followers thought of the goal of history in terms of "the Kingdom of God". But it is also plain that they saw the promises of the Lord of history and the expectations of Israel fulfilled in Jesus Himself. The day of the Lord had come. Jesus Christ the Messiah became the Central Fact of history, and the Revelatory Event in history, Who threw light upon both the past and future. Donald Baillie in *God Was in Christ,* put it like this:

From that central point faith could look backwards and forwards, and everything fell into its place in a sacred story whose center was the Christ who had come in the Flesh: Creation, Fall, Promise and Prophecy, the coming of Christ in the fulness of the time, His life and death and resurrection and ascension, the coming of the Holy Spirit, the Church and the spreading of the Gospel, the Second Coming and the final consummation. That is the Story that overcame the cyclic view of history, and it all depends on the Christology at the heart of it.[1]

This Christian theory of history can also be traced in the early church fathers such as Origen, Augustine and Tertullian, who launched spirited arguments against the cyclical doctrine and taught a new progressive, rectilinear view of history. To them Christ was the key to history, revealing its dynamics, its direction and its destiny.

[1] page 76.

It is then from this Judeo-Christian source that our Western world derived its belief in progress, and not from any classical tradition, or from an objective study of empirical evidence in history. It is a derivative of our faith, of our theology and Christology.

B

Next, *let us note what happened to this idea of progress, this belief in history as being meaningful and dynamic,* in the *succeeding centuries.* No great change came until the days of the Renaissance. According to Reinhold Niebuhr, "The Renaissance as a spiritual movement is best understood as a tremendous affirmation of the limitless possibilities of human existence, and as a rediscovery of the sense of a meaningful history."[1] It was more than a rebirth of learning in general and of classical learning in particular. It was "the rebirth of the earth and of human society. It was an expression of Christian eschatological hopes." It was a new attitude, an optimism, an affirmation towards the future and world history.

The "notions" of the Renaissance, as Stanley Romaine Hopper[2] points out, were essentially Christian "notions": that is, about the dignity of man, the rights of the individual, the importance of reason, and the meaningfulness of history. But two serious mistakes were made. First, these "notions" or beliefs were carried to an unwarranted extreme, which in the end made them false. And, secondly, they were divorced from their religious roots, and so became secular illusions, having no basis in reality, and their hopes no chance of realization, because they were a form of salvation without "grace". This was the beginning of a heretical movement which was to bear its bitter fruit in the spiritual crisis of our twentieth century.

On top of this revival of classical humanism, and the classical confidence in human capacities, there came Francis Bacon's *New Atlantis,* Thomas More's *Utopia,* Rene

[1] *Human Destiny,* page 160.
[2] *The Crisis of Faith,* Chapter 2.

159

Descartes' rationalism, Rousseau's naive nonsense about the natural goodness and perfectibility of human nature, the idealism of the French revolution, the optimism of European philosophers such as Condorcet, Fichte, Herder, Hegel, Croce and Comte. All of this, mind you, in a world of exploration, industrialization and steady expansion. Then, in 1859, came Charles Darwin's epoch-making book, *Origin of Species,* followed by the facile application of the doctrine of evolution, by many thinkers, to the social and historical process as well as to the biological world. And Herbert Spencer, more than any other writer, was responsible for the tendency "to convert doctrine of evolution into an instrument of unbridled optimism"[1].

Spencer stated his belief in this unqualified manner: "Always towards perfection is the mighty movement towards a complete development and a more unmixed good." Priestly was equally optimistic: "Nature, including both its materials and its laws, will be more at our command; men will make their situation in this world abundantly more easy and comfortable; they will prolong their existence in it and will grow daily more happy...Thus whatever the beginning of the world, the end will be glorious and paradisiacal beyond what our imagination can now conceive."[2]

Progress had now become much more than a possibility in the minds of Westerners. It had become a necessity — inevitable, determined, ultimate and automatic. "Every day and in every way," to quote Coue, "we were getting better and better." Mankind was astride a beneficent monster called evolution, which was taking him onwards and upwards to the Land of his fairest dreams. Even Christians were duped by this shallow and godless (the adjective is carefully chosen) optimism. One of the hymns to gain popularity was John Addington Symonds' "These things shall be..." whose fourth and sixth stanzas are:

[1]John Baillie in *The Belief in Progress,* page 144, 145.
[2]Quoted by Reinhold Niebuhr in *Human Destiny,* page 165.

Man shall love man, with heart as pure
And fervent as the young-eyed throng
Who chant their heavenly psalms before
God's face with undiscordant song.

There shall be no more sin, nor shame,
Though pain and passion may not die;
For men shall be at one with God
In bonds of firm necessity.

However, the climax came early in this century when certain philosophers went so far as to suggest that this progressive process even applied to God. He too was growing and developing. This concept is to be found in Henri Bergson's doctrine of "Creative Evolution", in William James' doctrine of a finite God and his "unfinished universe", in Lloyd Morgan's theory of "Emergent Evolution", and in Samuel Alexander's doctrine of Space-Time as being the single primordial matrix out of which the whole process of the universe emerges. Reality itself was evolving. God was Himself a product of evolution, or rather one day would be.

And, of course, if even God was subject to this law of progress so was everything else. Scholars saw in the Bible a progressive evolution of religious ideas and insights until they reached their purest in the Man of Galilee. The "ascent of man" culminated in Jesus, who was the crown and flower of humanity in its agelong upward struggle, and the supreme seeker and discoverer of God. Christianity itself was not a religion of Divine revelation, but the natural achievement of human genius and goodness.

C

Thirdly, *let us note the sudden drop from optimism to pessimism, from illusions to disillusionment.* Walter Lord, in *A Night to Remember,* a book on the sinking of the world's "unsinkable ship", the *Titanic,* in 1912, says that this event

161

symbolized the end of an era of confidence and the beginning of a new uneasy age. This is actually too much to claim for the sea disaster. But very soon afterwards there followed the First World War, then a universal economic depression, and then a Second World War which ended in the atomic blasts over Nagasaki and Hiroshima. Down crashed the idols of omnicompetent reason, human perfectibility, and inevitable progress, and with them disappeared our naive trust in technology, social organizations and governmental panaceas.

It was not till then that most of us moderns awoke to two tremendous truths which Christians always should have understood. The first one of these truths is about the ever-present reality of sin in human nature, and that it cannot be removed simply by knowledge and human achievement. People are more than rational or cognitive creatures. They are creatures of will and emotions — non-rational factors — and cannot be "saved" by education and secular culture. What looks like a humane and progressive society can at any moment be bedevilled by sin and egoism.

The second of these truths which we overlooked has to do with the ethical ambivalence of all man's powers and inventions. They are capable of being used for evil ends as well as for good ends. To quote Reinhold Niebuhr: "History cannot move forward towards increasing cosmos without developing possibilities of chaos by the very potencies which have enhanced cosmos."[1] For example, our airplanes and nuclear fission are neutral tools which can as easily be used for regress as for progress.

Western man has therefore been obliged to review history and discover where his thinking has gone off the rails. This has led him to find the trouble in Renaissance humanism and modern evolutionism. With the aid of prophets like Karl Barth, Emil Brunner, Reinhold Niebuhr, Paul Tillich and others, he has come to see the inherent falseness in divorcing

Human Destiny, page 169.

the Christian doctrine of a dynamic and meaningful history from the Christian Theology and Christology. The result is that today we have a better understanding of the Christian interpretation of history than at any time since the Reformation, if not since the days of Saint Augustine.

D

Let us now consider the nature of the Christian hope. It is a three-fold hope, and men always get into serious difficulties when they overlook or overemphasize any one of the three aspects of the doctrine of Christian eschatology.

1) First, *there is hope for individuals.* For immortality and heaven, of course, but also for a fullness of life in the here and now. We make a mistake in projecting the individual's only hope away off into a post-mortem state. And we make a far worse mistake in confining the fullness of life to the far-off event of a perfect society. That limits it to those future generations which would alone enjoy such a utopia, and makes all antecedent generations mere means in the historic process. But according to the New Testament human souls are the purpose and end of the story, so far as this world is concerned, and not just the servants of the species, or means to some other mundane end. Each generation is as important as any future generation. And the good life is within the grasp of each individual at any moment in history, and not just a privilege of a favoured few in some distant era. This is the way Herbert Butterfield, the great Cambridge historian, puts it: "If there is a meaning in history...it lies not in the systems and organizations that are built over long periods, but in something more essentially human, something in each personality...as an end in himself."[1]

Butterfield continues: "History is not like a train, the sole purpose of which is to get to its destination...If we want an analogy with history we must think of something like a

[1]Herbert Butterfield, *Christianity and History,* page 78.

Beethoven symphony — the point of it is not saved up until the end, the whole of it is not a mere preparation for a beauty that is only to be achieved in the last bar...each moment of it is its own self-justification, each note in its particular context as valuable as any other note...We envisage our history in the proper light, therefore, if we say that each generation — indeed each individual — exists for the glory of God."[1] "The purpose of history is not something that lies a thousand years ahead of us — it is constantly here, always with us, for ever achieving itself — the end of human history is the manufacture and education of human souls."[2]

Romain Rolland, the eminent French writer, states the same truth in these words: "So far as I am concerned, I have no need of this idol (worldly progress), because, for me the present comprises in itself the eternal. Salvation is not stowed away into an uncertain future; it is here, in the immediate present."[3]

And Robert Frost, the American poet, who put little stock in his fellow countrymen's chrome-plated dreams, shortly before his death, made this statement: "One can safely say after from six to thirty thousand years of experience that the evident design is a situation here in which it will always be equally hard to save your soul. Whatever progress may be taken to mean, it can't mean making the world any easier a place in which to save your soul."[4]

The Christian hope then includes the possibility of the good life for individuals in their own age, and in the immortal state.

2) Secondly, *there is the hope of the kingdom of God.* This kingdom is not man's but God's, it will not be "built" by man but is the gift of God, and it will not be fulfilled on this earth but beyond history. Hence it is not the climax of our

[1]Ibid, page 67.
[2]Ibid, page 76.
[3]Symposium: *Among the Great,* page 44.
[4]From a review in *Time* magazine.

social, economic, and political striving, a perfect society at the end of a long and progressive development, the apex of social evolution, as the Christian liberals of a few years ago were lead to believe.

The Kingdom of God means the rule of God. Therefore, it is moral and spiritual not political or material. It is the reign of God in men's hearts and lives, and in their social institutions, and not an earthly state which can one day be realized. *My Kingdom is not of this world,* said Jesus. Obviously, if what we have said earlier in this address is true, this kingdom or rule of God could never be fulfilled in human history, under the limitations of our finite and sinful state. Its consummation awaits the end of history. This is the crux of the doctrine of the Parousia or Second Advent.

But the New Testament also informs us that the kingdom or rule of God has already come — *This day is this fulfilled in your ears,* said Jesus, after He read in the synagogue Isaiah's description of the expected by-product of the coming of the kingdom. And over and over again He declared that the Kingdom they had been looking for had arrived — though its consummation was in the future, beyond history, its presence was actual, within history. God's rule had entered the historical process in the person of Jesus Christ, His Son, whose sinless life, mighty acts, vicarious death, and triumphant resurrection were evidence of the reign of God in power and glory.

This truth was proclaimed by C. H. Dodd in his famous doctrine of "realized eschatology", by Bishop Aulen in his book *Christus Victor,* by Walter Marshall Horton in *Our Eternal Contemporary,* and by Oscar Cullmann in several of his writings. Briefly, it means that God launched his D-Day against the powers of evil when He came in Christ, and that this is the pledge of His ultimate V-Day. Since Jesus is Lord He now rules as King, and a new age has come upon the world, the age of our Lord. This new age, according to Cullmann is the kingdom of Christ, and is destined to continue until the end of earthly history, when it will give place to the kingdom of God, which will then appear in all its full power and glory.

3) Thirdly, *there is hope for human history.* Since Christ has come and rules as King, the historical process in this age of our Lord is pregnant with possibilities of hope and redemption. And although the kingdom of God is not a social order it is always relevant to the social order — God's rule should be realized in our economic, political and social institutions; the kingdoms of this world should become the kingdom of our Lord and His Christ. This is the aspect of the Christian hope which is neglected or denied by the pietistic sects which concern themselves only with Beulah Land, and by the pre-millennialists who are busily engaged in calculating the date of the end of the world, or preening their feathers and waiting for Jesus to come on the clouds and whisk them off to the city four-square with its 144,000 inhabitants.

As I understand it, the Christian hope for history can be delineated best by making several observations. The first of them is: *A perfect society on earth is never a possibility.* Because of human pride and sin, and the ethical ambivalence in all our knowledge and powers, we can never achieve more than partial justice and partial righteousness. Man must always live under the tension created by his infinite aspirations and his finite limitations. Instead of progress being inevitable or automatic, every moment in history is open to regress and chaos. The word "Utopia" is a Latin word meaning "No place". A perfect society is not in the cards. Like every past age in human history, every future age will also be fouled up.

The second Christian hope is that *change should not be equated with progress.* True progress must be ethical and spiritual. As it is possible for human beings to become "better off" without becoming "better", so it is possible for human societies to attain a higher standard of living, a more equal distribution of "goods and services", a greater measure of economic and social liberation, and yet become morally decadent, spiritually empty and meaningless, and socially bland.

Northrop Frye, in his book *The Modern Century,* warns that what we call "progress" could easily lead to mass culture with homogenized citizens, uniform and monotonous like sheep or ants, instead of varied and rich in their individualism; to a gradual loss of a sense of personal responsibility and a prevalence of mob rule; and to bankruptcy in spiritual as well as personal values and the dominance of a crass materialism and amoral populism.

And Jacques Ellul, in *The Presence of the Kingdom* (page 199), writes: "I refuse to believe in the 'progress' of humanity when I see from year to year the lowering of standards among men I know...when I see them weighed down by anxiety...by fear...by hatred..., when I see them cowered by circumstances, and as they suffer, becoming thieves and frauds, embittered, avaricious, selfish, unbelieving, full of resentment and rancour."

We may make the world a more liveable place for more of God's children, but even our best economic and social solutions will not answer man's deepest needs, and will carry their own possibilities of evil.

However, *we must still believe that progress is always a possibility.* Because we repudiate a belief in its inevitability, and refuse to equate material and political improvements with true progress, does not mean that we should either belittle worldly progress, or lose hope in spiritual progress. History is still a place where God acts, and it is therefore dynamic and meaningful. There are encouraging signs of this in our present age. For example, there is a new conscience on war, on racism, and on poverty. There is a new sense of man's interdependence, both at home in our programmes to assist the needy in the nation, and in our global

167

attempts to create new systems of justice and co-operation. There are signs of a new awareness of the earthly environment, of self-determination for women, blacks, and nations formerly under colonial rule, and of a more human and responsible international economic order.

Christians should be realists but not pessimists. There are enough doomsday writers without us. The note of despair runs through the writings of Beckett, Ionesco, Albee and most of the great modern playwrights. Some of our eminent scholars are predicting that the world is on a decline, and that we may be approaching the end of what we call "our civilization". Others are writing doom-and-gloom tales about the earth being overwhelmed by insects (*The Hillstrom Chronicle*), by plague (*The Omega Man*), by pollution (*No Blade of Grass*), by people (*Z.P.G.*, "Zero Population Growth"), by apes (*The Planet of the Apes*), and by violence (*A Clockwork Orange*). There is no present scarcity of dystopias!

But troubles and problems do not make our age unique or different from any other. Listen to this: "I am sick of life, if this life can be called life...(there are) no hopes of any improvement...the age is Satan's own; gladly would I see myself and all my people snatched from it." That was written by Martin Luther in the 16th century. And yet if we believe the Bible, we must believe that God is the Lord of history, and in Jesus Christ He has entered the historical process and struck a fatal blow at the powers of darkness, and established His own reign of righteousness. There may be few clear signs of His victory, and certainly we are not on an ascending escalator moving steadily upward with no stops or reverses. But as long as God lives, hope must not die.

> *Almighty Father, who dost give*
> *The gift of life to all who live,*
> *Look down on all earth's sin and strife,*
> *And lift us to a nobler life.*

Lift up our hearts, O King of Kings,
To brighter hopes and kindlier things,
To visions of a larger good,
And holier dreams of brotherhood.

FOUR

A NEW HEAVEN AND A NEW EARTH

And I saw a new heaven and a new earth: for the first heaven and the first earth were passed away; and there was no more sea. And I, John, saw the holy city, new Jerusalem, coming down from God out of heaven.

Revelation 21: 1,2.

From time immemorial men have vied with each other in their attempts to portray, and even delineate, a perfect society, a new earth, where there would be "no more sea" of trouble and sorrow, poverty and ignorance, oppression and war, sin and death. To this end Plato wrote his *Republic,* Augustine his *City of God,* Francis Bacon his *New Atlantis,* and Thomas More his *Utopia.* However, the most famous vision of the good society is John the Divine's "New Jerusalem" described in Chapter 21 of the book of Revelation.

There is a popular fallacy that John's picture is of the heavenly kingdom. But he plainly tells us that the "New Jerusalem" will come down from heaven, and will be established upon the earth. It will endure for a thousand years, and then the whole earthly frame of things will dissolve, and the true kingdom of God will be realized in heaven, and will continue for ever. The "New Jerusalem" is not the final home of the blessed but the ideal earthly society.

Until we understand the purpose of John's writing, we

are inclined to think that he is overly concerned with materialistic images of splendour and magnificence. He piles them high — silver, gold, marble, precious stones, rivers, gardens, and fountains — and seems to be oblivious to moral and spiritual values. But we should remember that his picture owes much to the *Genesis* account of the Garden of Eden, the mythological first perfect society, and to the proud, extravagant city of Rome which was persecuting him and his fellow Christians. John is predicting that Rome will be brought low, and will be replaced by another earthly city which will far excel it in glory. In a day of darkness and cruel treatment this is a vision of a new and better day. It is a message of hope in a time of despair.

A

Well, *a new earth is our dream too — yours, mine and everybody's.* We live in an age when the sword of Damocles hangs threateningly over every nation, and when the clouds of pessimism darken the sky over every continent. And we dream of a future of justice, peace and brotherhood. *But* — and here is the point I wish to stress today — *what we need first is not a new earth but a new heaven.* John's order is correct: *A new heaven and a new earth.* It is the new heaven which precedes and produces the new earth.

Here we touch the crucial flaw in all secular utopias. They are to be the product of men's efforts and genius, and will presumably arise man-made from down here below. They are to be practical, brave solutions for all the world's ills, without any reference to or dependence upon a Higher Power, or intangible values. But their end is frustration and disaster. We will not, and we cannot, get a new earth without first getting a new heaven.

This is the main point in the story of Jesus' temptations in the wilderness. The devil suggested that He might turn the stones into bread and become an economic messiah, and solve

171

the problems of poverty and hunger; and that He might take over the rule of earthly kingdoms and become a political messiah, and solve the problems of oppression and war. You may be sure that these temptations were very real and powerful to Jesus, because He wished people, all people, to have a better life on the material and social levels, and He saw the great need for a new society of justice, prosperity, freedom and peace. But He saw also that this was the devil's attempt to divert Him from His essential mission and reduce Him to a reformer. Mankind's primary need was a new heaven, and this was the challenge and dimension of Jesus' ministry.

The Nazis had a cynical saying, "Leave the sky to the sparrows." But when we do that, it is not long before the sky is taken over by the hawks and vultures. That is exactly what happened in Germany. The basic evil of Nazism was that their heaven was all wrong. It was filled with cruel, pagan gods, and all kinds of corrupt values and standards. And instead of creating a new earth, it revived an old earth of tyranny, hatred, fear and war.

And so the crisis of our century is basically a spiritual crisis — theological not economic, political or ideological. Our heaven is all wrong, and as a consequence our earth is all wrong too. Not until our vertical relationship is put right can our horizontal relationships be corrected. It is because of the recognition of this fundamental truth that we in the United Church of Canada have a department of Evangelism and Social Action. This order must not be reversed, as Christian liberalism with its social Gospel often tends to do. Nor should it be emasculated, as Christian orthodoxy with its personal Gospel would sometimes like to have it. Christianity is neither a secular humanitarianism nor an irrelevant pietistic individualism. It is both otherworldly and worldly, and in that order. The social Gospel needs a theology, and the personal Gospel needs a social ethic.

B

The basic question of our age, as of every age, is the God-question. If we were asked to check the Ten Commandments and put them in order of importance, many of us would put the commandments forbidding murder, adultery, and theft at or near the top. Great prophetic religion knew better. It had the insight to understand that the God-question must be settled first, before any other question can be satisfactorily settled. And so the first commandment is this: *Thou shalt have no other gods before me.* And when Jesus was requested to name the greatest commandment, He answered: *The first of all the commandments is...Thou shalt love the Lord thy God...this is the first commandment. And the second is like, namely this, Thou shalt love thy neighbour as thyself. (Mark 12:29-31)*

Our age is corrupt and confused and critical because it is idolatrous. Man's heart is sick because it is promiscuous. Man's feet are aimless because they are wandering. Man's soul is impoverished because it is unfaithful. Modern man may profess belief in the God and Father of our Lord Jesus Christ, but his service and allegiance are given to false gods. Old gods, as someone has said, like old soldiers never die, or even fade away, but lurk in their corners waiting to crowd in upon the empty or wavering soul. Nature abhors a vacuum, and the human soul, like the haunted house in Jesus' parable, will not remain empty, but will be invaded by brazen idols. Witness the universal popularity today of such old pagan gods as Venus, the God of Physical pleasure; Aphrodite, the goddess of love, sex and sensuality; Apollo, the god of the body and bodily health; and Irene, the goddess of peace and tranquillity. But even more serious is our modern allegiance to such false gods as Mammon, Caesar, Demos and Vulcan. Our earth is all wrong because our heaven is filled with these pagan gods.

There is Mammon, the god of money and material

173

things, prosperity and personal success. John Milton, in *Paradise Lost,* warns that Mammon is "The least-erected spirit that fell from Heaven," but that he always pleases the throng. They may not believe or even understand a philosophical materialism, but they subscribe to a practical, everyday materialism. Modern man's chief end appears to be to heap up riches, to tear down his barns and build greater, to provide himself with the means and comforts of materialistic living, and to attain economic security on an affluent gilt-edged scale. Money is our divinity. The manner of getting it is immaterial. Get it! That is what counts. And those who do get it are those who measure up to our standard of success and greatness, and receive our approbation and imitation. Not only business and industry but politics, education, and even religion have been conscripted into the service of Great God Mammon. Like the Israelites in Moses' absence, we have made ourselves a Golden Calf and given it our devotion.

Some years ago when I was minister of Robertson United Church, Edmonton, Alberta, I received a slip from the Home Missions Department in Toronto informing me of a young immigrant's forthcoming arrival in Edmonton. On the line which told of his "Church Affiliation" was typed "Bank of Montreal". A slight error in typing? Yes...But for most of us fundamentally a correct answer to the question of "Church Affiliation".

Secondly, *there is Caesar, the god of the State and narrow nationalism.* The famous historian, Arnold J. Toynbee, declared that nationalism "has very largely superseded Christianity as the religion of the Western World." This idolatry can be seen in every country. It has its sacred days and sacred symbols, its loyalty oaths and heresy trials, its shrines and prophets. In some countries it purges the literature, the school textbooks, and even the Church's sermons, to bring them into line with its idolatrous doctrine, and it disciplines or liquidates those who will not conform. In most countries its devotees sing the national anthem with much more fervor and attention than they sing any hymn to the Lord God of Hosts, and treat the national flag with much more reverence than they do the cross of our Lord Jesus Christ. And most countries demand total allegiance of their citizens, even to the point of life itself.

Is it any wonder that in our century we have been devastated by wars of unprecedented totality and destruction? We have been trapped in the anarchic battle of the tribal pagan gods.

Thirdly, *there is Demos, the god of democracy.* A few years ago that incisive observer of contemporary life, Reinhold Niebuhr, wrote in his paper "Christianity and Crisis", after he had heard or read a number of speeches delivered at college graduation exercises: "If one may judge by the various commencement utterances,...Americans have only one religion: devotion to democracy. They extol its virtues, are apprehensive about the perils to which it is exposed, pour maledictions upon its foes, rededicate themselves periodically to its purposes, and claim unconditioned validity for its ideals. Does not the very extravagance of our devotion prove that we live in a religiously vapid age, in which even Christians fail to penetrate to the more ultimate issues of life?"

We Westerners need Dr. Niebuhr's warning, because we are constantly in danger of identifying democracy with Christianity, and turning our churches into agents for promotion and preservation. In fact many of the appeals presented to people to allay themselves with the Church have nothing profound to say about God or Jesus Christ or the Gospel of Salvation, but are geared to man's loyalty to democracy and our "Way of Life". God and Christ and the Church are just servants to the Great God Demos.

Two speeches that I heard recently in Ontario illustrate this point. The first one was by a teacher of teachers in this province, who said that Christianity and democratic citizenship were to him synonymous. The second one was by a well-known university professor, who frankly told us that he was not a churchman, and added, "My religion is democracy." This is arrant and ignorant nonsense. Democracy itself has its roots in the Christian conception of God, and its very survival depends upon its subservience and accountability to Him.

Fourthly, *there is Vulcan, the god of Science and tools,* a very capable, omnipresent and omnicompetent god. His products are all about us, and very impressive: automation, airplanes, motor cars, television, X-rays, penicillin, electricity, indoor plumbing, and scientific agriculture. The march of science in the last half-century has been a thrilling one, and most of us have a supreme confidence in our new gadgets and vaccines and wonder-drugs. By our research and inventions we are going to create a chrome-plated, foam-rubber society free from disease, poverty, ignorance and strife. A modern paraphrase of *Psalm 23* begins like this, "Science is my Shepherd, I shall not want," and continues with the word "science" replacing the words "The Lord" throughout.

Now science, like democracy or the state or money, is a very great value, but when it becomes an idol we get the religion of scientism, religion of human self-sufficiency, which worships the creature instead of the Creator, and which not only tries to control all human life but to interpret it in naturalistic terms. God becomes unnecessary to the running and explaining of His universe.

But what about Nagasaki and Hiroshima? What about the carnage and destruction of two world wars? What about the slums and anonymity, the pollution and wastage, the tensions and neuroses of our drug and aspirin age? These are a long way from the desires of the pure scientist. Here is the nature and depth of our predicament. The most ingenious and efficient creations of man's scientific "know-how" have been turned against the creator. Because they cannot manage the human element in the equation, they cannot direct motives,

176

create values or control objectives. They are only neutral tools. Unless God comes first, our science may destroy us and blast the earth into ashes and debris.

C

Let us now see where our idolatry has brought us. The Psalmist, many centuries ago, wrote, *Their sorrows shall be multiplied that hasten after another god.* It was, alas, a prediction which was bound to come true. Back in the 1950's Aldous Huxley wrote a novel called *The Devils of Loudun,* which was reviewed in the *New York Times* under the heading, "False Gods and the Devil to Pay". A modern writer, commenting on this heading, said, "We live in the kind of universe where a man's moral and spiritual orientation brings its own reward and exacts its own price. There is the devil to pay when we no longer worship the one God...and begin to render homage and devotion to lesser gods."

Our age clearly and decisively illustrates the truth of that statement. The deadly malaise threatening the life of modern civilization is a spiritual disease known as idolatry, which starts at the heart of humanity and eats away until all the vital organs are diseased. When we are wrong about our God, we are defective all along the line. When our heaven is filled with pagan gods, there will be the devil to pay on our earth.

For example, *false gods give us a false set of values.* The cheap and transient, the secondary and relative values are raised to first place, and the eternal values are devaluated and reduced to luxuries or trifles. This is only natural because eternal values do not come out of thin air, or from low-vaulted heavens. They are not the creation of the false gods of materialism, nationalism, democracy or science. It would be folly to expect Truth, Beauty and Goodness from a heaven whose gods are idols.

Our modern world is bankrupt of these spiritual values, which alone can give dignity, meaning and purpose to human life, and which alone are worthy objectives for our striving. We live in a "Sensate culture", a "Prodigal Son Culture", a country far away from the Father's treasures. This can be seen in our modern literature, music, art, and drama which are obsessed with the earthy and sensual, and are devoid of any accents or overtones of spiritual values, or eternal realities.

Again, *false gods give us false moral codes.* In fact, they abolish morals altogether; and replace them with axioms of expediency. Without the Absolute God there can be no absolute morality. The queston of "Which is right?" gives way to "Which is desirable?" There is no justice or truth in the ultimate sense, because there is no ultimate ground for them, no Holy God, and each false god claims the right (of a god) to dictate its own moral code for its own particular domain. And so Great God Mammon pontifically affirms "Business is business;" and Great God Caesar, "My country, right or wrong;" Great God Demos, "The voice of the people is the voice of God;" and Great God Vulcan, "Man is the measure of all things."

The result of course is moral anarchy, a state of chaos, where there is only one criterion — advantage. Silence the minorities, assassinate character, exploit the helpless, clamber to success on the backs of the oppressed, pollute the air and the water, destroy the environment, launch an aggressive war against a smaller nation, turn the fruits of research into bombs for civilian targets — who can call you to account? Not the gods whose orders you are carrying out. And the earth is ravished!

Or again, *false gods give us a false view of ourselves and our fellowmen.* There is only one God who can give us a belief in the sacredness of human personality, and that is the Father of us all. In the eyes of the false gods we are only atoms or animals, blood plasma or cannon fodder, hands or cogs, cyphers or robots. Do we wonder that millions of human

178

beings have, in these past sixty years, been sacrificed on the bloody altar of these pagan gods? Never has there been a more wholesale devaluation of persons. We have seen the common man becoming all the commoner by being robbed of his high-born dignity, and reduced to a thing without ultimate worth or inherent rights. If our heaven has no Father-God, our earth can have no spiritual children — just clods and grasshoppers.

And finally, *false gods give us false goals.* They draw blueprints for "new orders" of their own, and say, "All these things will I give thee if thou wilt fall down and worship me." Wise men know that that is the platform on which Satan hopes to rise to power, and that it can only bring them ruin, but there are always enough dupes who will rally round the standards of the idols, prepared to serve them with zeal, and to launch a "holy crusade" in pursuit of their objectives. And so we have millions of volunteers in the scramble for a gold-plated security, or a Marxist society, or a national place in the sun.

And there is the devil to pay! To achieve their goals it is necessary to beat their plowshares into swords and their pruning hooks into spears, to stimulate their economic systems and rally their propaganda machines, and to make one last mad dash for Utopia. Heels together, quick march, drums in front, off we go, with guns instead of butter, bombs instead of bread, lies instead of truth, and regimentation instead of freedom. Blood is spilled, women are raped, little children are slain in their beds, cities are wiped out, green fields are devastated, nations ravaged, inflation mounts, starvation becomes epidemic, and the world resembles Inferno more than Paradise.

And the whole secret of our predicament is that we have not solved the god-question. Not until we do shall we get an eternal set of values, a valid moral order, a sacred estimate on human beings, and a worthy goal for all our striving. *Seek ye first the Kingdom of God and His righteousness,* said Jesus, *and all these things* (justice, brotherhood, peace) *will be added unto you* — as by-products of your new loyalty and devotion.

And I saw a new heaven and a new earth: for the first heaven and the first earth were passed away; and there was no more sea. And I, John, saw the holy city, new Jerusalem, coming down from God out of heaven.

A NEW HEAVEN AND A NEW EARTH!

The Very Reverend Angus J. MacQueen